MW00628826

The Boy Who
Survived

Other books by Alton Carter

The Boy Who Carried Bricks

Aging Out

The Boy Who Dreamed Big

The Boy Who Went to the Library

The Boy Who Survived

A True Story of
Hope and Resilience

Alton Carter

THE ROADRUNNER PRESS
OKLAHOMA CITY, OKLAHOMA

Published by The RoadRunner Press
Oklahoma City, Oklahoma
www.TheRoadRunnerPress.com

© 2019 by Alton Carter
Cover © 2019 The RoadRunner Press
All rights reserved.

Cover Illustration: Thomas Hilley
Cover design by Jeanne Devlin
Journal art by Janelda Lane

The RoadRunner Press is committed to publishing works of quality
and integrity. The story, the experiences, and the words shared here
are the author's alone. Some names have been changed
out of respect for those who lived this story.

Printed in the USA
First edition: December 2019
For special bulk, group, or custom orders,
please contact: orders@theroadrunnerpress.com or call 405.524.6205.

Library of Congress Control Number: 2019941662

Publisher's Cataloging-In-Publication Data
(Prepared by The Donohue Group, Inc.)

Names: Carter, Alton, author.
Title: The boy who survived : a true story of resilience / Alton Carter.
Description: First edition. | Oklahoma City, Oklahoma : The RoadRunner
Press, 2019. | Interest age level: 13 and up. | Summary: "Alton Carter, a former
foster child and police officer, shares more stories of survival and hope from
his life"--Provided by publisher.
Identifiers: ISBN 9781937054915 (hardcover) | ISBN 9781937054946 (trade
paper) | ISBN 9781950871032 (ebook)
Subjects: LCSH: Carter, Alton--Juvenile literature. | African American men--Bi-
ography--Juvenile literature. | African American youth--Social conditions--Ju-
venile literature. | Foster children--Biography--Juvenile literature. | CYAC:
Carter, Alton. | African Americans--Biography. | African Americans--Social
conditions. | Foster children--Biography. | LCGFT: Autobiographies.
Classification: LCC E185.97.C37 A3 2019 (print) | LCC E185.97.C37 (ebook) |
DDC 305.896073/092 B--dc23

10 9 8 7 6 5 4 3 2

*To my wife, Kristin, who has stood by me
through thick and thin, and my children—Kelton, Colin,
Alliyah, Angilina, and Curtis—who have shown me
what unconditional love looks like*

People ask why I share my story
over and over with complete strangers.
It's because I want to provide
hope for those who feel alone, and
I don't know what else to do with it.

— Alton

Chapter 1

Hindsight

As I look back and reflect on my childhood, I see one thing painfully clear: my family doing what they can to make sure the cycle of dysfunction continues.

My father is missing in action long before I am born, leaving me with a lifetime of unanswered questions.

My mother is raising five children on her own, while battling a deep depression and a crippling addiction.

My uncles are all cautionary tales.

My grandparents are enablers.

I can see now that my mother is stronger than she knows, but every house we live in is in shambles and almost always riddled with roaches. The state has given my mother more chances than she deserves before finally removing my siblings and me from her custody and then placing us in the home of my grandparents, her parents.

My grandparents' house on Third Street in the university town of Stillwater, Oklahoma, is nothing more than a change of address—occupied by four or more adults on any given day battling drug addiction or alcohol addiction or both.

I see all this now as clearly as I see my face in the mirror. And I fear for the little boy I was.

And although I know he is a survivor and so, like his mother, stronger than he knows, I also know the world will not see him as one for many years to come.

I am the boy who survived.

And I now know what he and so many children like him don't know: that this is a daily decision, a daily decision not to surrender to the pain and fear swirling all around you—string enough of those days together and you become resilient, able to withstand neglect, abuse, homelessness, shame, hunger, and fear, trials that would knock a grown man to his knees.

Resilience
re-sil-ience
noun
: the capacity to recover quickly from
  difficulties; toughness

: an ability to recover from or adjust easily
  to misfortune and change

: the capability of a strained body to
  recover its size and shape after

deformation caused especially by
compressive stress

* * *

My grandmother, like her daughter, battled what in
her day they called the blues. She also spent way too
much time covering for the misdeeds of the three adult
Carter sons who lived with her and Grandpa. My grandfather was a man of integrity in a family that did not
value honor, but by refusing to buck Grandma, he also
enabled her—allowing her to enable their grown sons.

Yet Grandpa provided my first hope.

He offered me a glimpse of another way to live. He
often worked three jobs without complaint, doing what
he could to feed the dozen or more souls living under his
roof on any given day.

Ironically, I hated to see him leave for work, but that
was because I felt safe only when he was around. I eagerly
awaited his return each evening, and not until I was back
in his presence could I put the day behind me. That held
true for years—no matter how hard my day or what troubles followed me home from school.

Yes, I idolized my grandfather. He was a good, honest,
hardworking man. He was also the only person in my
family who saw *me* . . . the only person who saw *the good
in me*.

Grandpa believed in me.

He believed I could be more, do more. That let me
believe I could too. My grandfather gave me hope that

maybe I could have a better life someday. Looking back, I now realize that hope is the water that resilience needs to grow. And he gave me my first drop.

So you might be surprised to learn that the three years I lived with my grandparents were a nightmare. Or if you're a fellow survivor, not surprised at all. One person—sometimes the same person—can bring sunshine or storm to a home on any given day, sometimes any given hour. My life could change with the opening of the front door, when instead of my grandfather, my Uncle Stevie came through the door.

I lived in constant fear of that particular uncle, and the fact that sometimes he could also be the warm sun of my world—the uncle who would joke or play with us—made the times he became the storm all the more terrifying.

I was only a first-grader, but I already knew that people's faces are like a wood fence: You never know what's going on behind them.

The first person outside my family that I ever trusted was my fourth-grade teacher, Brenda Thompson. She took me in when no other teacher wanted me and told me the truth when I did not want to hear it, kindly, but frankly. In doing so, she sent me the message that I could handle the truth—something that fake platitudes could never do.

And so, thanks to her, my resilience grew some more.

During my fourth-grade year, I gained the courage to stand up to my Uncle Stevie, an act that brought no applause or praise but instead cost me my family. I can still see that night all these years later, unfolding like a bad home movie: I refuse to ever again drink the whiskey he plied my siblings, cousins, and me with at night, often on school nights. And he throws me down a staircase.

I call 9-1-1, and the police come—as you count on them to do in your time of need. They haul my uncle away as my grandmother curses them from the front yard. The police pull away, and my grandmother turns her wrath on me.

The pain of my bruised ribs from my fall that night was nothing compared to the damage her tongue-lashing did to my heart. Grandmothers are supposed to protect their little grandchildren, not reject them.

I knew that even if Grandma had forgotten.

That night, I walked away from my grandparents' believing that I had no other option and convinced that the house on Third Street could no longer be my home. I spent the next ten years being shuffled between foster and children's homes—never feeling truly wanted, always missing my siblings and cousins, and often feeling guilty for having left them behind in that field of land mines we called home.

Many of the places where I took refuge or shelter came with some form of neglect or abuse, but I decided early on that anything was better than living with my biological family.

And I still believe that to be true.

Neglect and abuse are always harmful, but the harm cuts deeper when delivered by the people who are supposed to love you.

My Story

The Boy Who Carried Bricks
is a story of my life
Chapters of abuse
that cut like a knife

Left all alone
hungry and afraid
Bugs crawled the walls
our bills never paid

I needed her love
more than air
It didn't seem to matter
she didn't seem to care

She often went away
without saying goodbye
I watched her leave
she watched me cry

I dreamed of more
than what we had
I wanted to be different
I wished for a dad

I dreamed of an angel
both night and day
That someone would come
and take me away

When the judge said *enough*
betrayal came to town
To grandparents I went
in whiskey I would drown

I knew it wasn't right
hurt me I don't care
I refuse to be like him
I tumbled down the stairs

Left you all behind
I took the pain you gave
It's hard to be alone
my life I had to save

To the ranch I went
living with the man of God
Abusive as the rest
I found this sadly odd

He made me call him Dad
those words hurt my head
I'm a sinner who needs saving
that is what he said

I crawled upon the ground
the man was full of tricks
He screamed hateful things
I carried loads of bricks

ALTON CARTER

The church watched me suffer
a deacon he became
Cuss me, then pray
the man had no shame

In Ag I felt accepted
my teacher cared no doubt
He made me feel worthwhile
when others left me out

They fired the deacon
for what he had done
He deserved what he got
not his wife and son

When I had enough
I ran when I could
No more carrying bricks
no more hauling wood

Moved on to Boyle
in the middle of the sticks
A house on the corner
that also sat on bricks

The town was small
I didn't fit in
We had nothing in common
but the color of our skin

Now I know
I'm not like others
I'll never be accepted
thanks to my mother

Cushing called for me
so a Tiger I became
Different town, different place
but the same old game

Isolated at first
alone for awhile
I came alive
when they fixed my smile

Sports changed it all
I loved playing the game
I helped the team win
now they know my name

Chapter 2

Mosquito Bites

Normally, Mom took the tiny pink pills several times a day, which then made her sleep a lot despite the sun being out.

Nights were different.

Mom rarely slept and was often irritable. And for whatever reason, I seemed to irritate her the most. It's not that I was a bad kid, but I was not like my siblings either. I was hyperactive, emotional, and always hungry. I was also blessed—or you could say cursed—with the gift of constantly opening my mouth at the wrong time.

I think that is why Mom's anger usually fell on me.

I can't say our relationship was always like that, but certainly by the age of eight, I was aware that Mom was annoyed by almost everything I did. One night stands out in particular.

As I remember it, we were home for summer vacation in the middle of June. We had little in the house to eat, and Mom had failed to pay the electric bill. No electricity in an Oklahoma summer meant any food in the refrigerator was spoiling fast and any baths taken would be in cold water. We had finished our baths, put on our makeshift pajamas of underwear and T-shirts, and taken our places on what served as our bed—a few blankets thrown on the living-room floor.

We had done this all in the dark.

The house was still so hot my sleeping shirt was already soaked in sweat. Even the slightest of breezes would have been welcome, but with no electricity, there could be no whirling fan to move around the heavy air, and we could not open the windows because of the mosquitoes.

I tried to go to sleep, truly I did, but I was so darn miserable. I tossed and turned, and then to make matters worse, my stomach began to growl. I knew better than to ask for something to eat, but when I saw the shadowy figure of Mom passing by, I couldn't help myself.

"Mom, can I have something to eat?"

Mom stopped and, without saying a word, started toward me. I quickly sputtered, "I'm sorry! Never mind!" My apology came too late.

"Why can't you lay down and go to sleep like your brothers and sisters?" she hissed.

I had no answer for her.

"You're always crying and complaining about nothing," she muttered. "I'm going to give you something to teach you a lesson."

In one swift motion, Mom grabbed me and dragged me to the front door.

"I'm sorry! I'm sorry!" I cried.

My pleading was too little too late. Mom knew how hot it was outside; she knew I was hungry. Yet in that moment, neither seemed to matter to her.

"You're a crybaby who never appreciates anything." Those were the second-to-last words I heard from her before she opened the front door and pushed me out onto the front porch. Her final words would stay with me always: "I don't want to look at you anymore!"

With that, Mom slammed the front door shut.

I immediately proved the truth of her words by plopping down on the small cement porch and beginning to cry, hoping all the while that the sound of my sobs would persuade my mother to open the door and let me back inside the house.

When I realized they would not, I began to berate myself: *Why couldn't I have just laid on the floor and gone to sleep like my brothers and sister?*

Why doesn't Mom like me?

Ouch! I slapped my arm.

My jumble of thoughts had been interrupted by the bite of a hungry mosquito that flew away unfazed.

A few minutes later I was bit again—and then again and again. Convinced that I now had a good reason for my mom to let me back inside, I knocked on the front door. "Mom, the mosquitoes are biting me. I promise I won't complain anymore if you'll let me back in. I will be good and go right to sleep—let me in!"

I can't tell you how long I stood there knocking and begging to be let back in the house, but it felt like forever.

The door remained closed.

At some point, I gave up.

If my news about the mosquitoes hadn't made her open the door, crying and continuing to knock much longer would only make her mad. And the last thing I wanted was for her anger to grow.

I sank to the porch floor and felt the mosquitoes return one by one. I drew my legs to my chest and pulled my oversized T-shirt over them. This kept the mosquitoes off my legs, but left my head, arms, and back bare and vulnerable. I stayed hunkered down like that until the sun appeared, chasing the swarm of mosquitoes away and revealing angry mosquito bites all over my body.

The temperature was also rising fast.

I started to sweat; the mosquito bites began to itch. The bites seemed to be everywhere, and I soon realized I couldn't scratch in a thousand places at the same time. Just when I thought I couldn't take the itching anymore, Mom opened the front door. She took one look at me and told me to go get in the bathtub.

I raced to the bathroom—scratching all the way. I filled the bathtub with water, cold water, that being all we had. I scrubbed everywhere I could reach with soap, and then dripping wet, I climbed out of the tub.

Mom was waiting for me with a cotton swab and calamine lotion. She dipped the swab in the lotion and then dabbed it on a mosquito bite or three. She did this until every bite had been tended to.

Then she handed me my clothes and told me to get dressed. Those were her only words for me.

And then she left.

I sat there—perched on the edge of the bathtub, my body dotted in pink lotion—hurting and wondering why my mother hadn't shown the slightest sign of sympathy for me or remorse for her part in my pain.

The Past
It's all about the past
And past is all you got
Your past is full of wounds
It hurts like you've been shot
Your dream contains memories
And moments you never had
Your dreams are broken and empty
Your dreams are mostly sad
So if your dreams are painful
And they take away your voice
Create the dreams you hope for
Remember you have a choice

Chapter 3

Mama's Got a Gun

Trying to raise five young children on her own had taken its toll on Mom, but on one particular day, she seemed more agitated than normal. Every little thing we did drew a face slap or a whipping—responses that far outweighed the wrongdoing.

Before long, my siblings and I gathered up what few toys we had and headed outside to the small patch of grass we called our front yard to get away from the anger.

Mom stayed inside.

As the hours passed, we grew sweaty and thirsty. I wanted to go indoors for a drink of water and to get out of the hot sun, and I'm sure my sister and brothers did too, but not a one of us dared to try. We had learned long ago—without a word ever being said—to never risk going inside when Mom was having one of her bad days.

Mom took pills that were supposed to make the bad days go away, but they did not always work. This was one of those days.

So, instead, we took turns drinking from the low faucet on the side of the house and tried to ignore our rumbling tummies until the night finally drove us back inside. We filed into the house single file and then each of us took a seat on the living room floor—still in the dark.

Yes, the electricity was off again.

The house was filthy as usual too—and even though we couldn't see in the dark, we could feel the roaches scurrying about on the floor. No one dared move, however. Nobody said a word either—we knew better than to do so when Mom was having one of her bad days.

When Mom finally joined us in the living room, however, all seemed well. Maybe that's what gave my brother the courage to ask for something to eat. We hadn't eaten all day, but Mom reacted as if a switch had been flipped.

"There is no food!" she screamed.

Five little heads ducked into our shoulders like turtles pulling back into their shells.

"I haven't paid the electric bill. I haven't paid the rent!" Mom screamed. And then she screamed the scariest thing of all. "They're going to kick us out of our house!"

Her screams pierced the dark like bullets of fear. With each shout, her fury seemed to grow. One by one, she picked each of us up, gave us a shake, and then slammed us down on the old dirty couch like discarded rag dolls. When she grabbed me—and just before she slammed me down—I looked into her face, and I did not recognize my mother. Rage had so consumed her that every muscle had tightened until her face looked like a scary mask, not the mother I loved. I had seen Mom mad before plenty of times but never like this, and for the first time in my life, I was afraid of her.

She left us on the couch, sitting in a row like ducks in an arcade game, and went to the bedroom, the only bedroom in the house. Instead of going to bed like usual, however, she stormed back into the living room—only this time hiding something in her hand as she screamed about what bad and ungrateful children we were.

We huddled on the couch, shaking with fear, while Mom paced back and forth in front of us, always keeping the one hand hidden from view.

As her pace quickened, she began to tell us in harsh detail how we had ruined her life.

She could not keep a man because of us.
She could not work because of us.
She could not pay the bills because of us.
She had no friends because of us.
We were horrible, horrible children.
And she would be better off without us.

Then, when her fury seemed spent, she planted herself in front of us. She pulled the hand she had kept hidden from behind her back and revealed the gun it held.

We did not move.

I watched in fear as she pointed the gun at the ceiling. Releasing another horrible scream, she then leaned in close and stuck the small black gun in each of our faces one by one.

"I'm not afraid to die," she said. "I ought to just kill all of you and then kill myself."

She was no longer screaming, and somehow, that gave her words more power.

She slowly straightened and put the gun to her temple. She stood like that for what felt like forever. Years would pass before I remembered this moment—my brain's attempt to protect me, I suppose. A child is not built to see his mother in such despair. Neither is a man. And now that I have recalled the most desperate night of my childhood, I know I will never forget it.

Time slowed to a stop.

With the pistol still to her head, Mom stood over us, an empty look in her eyes.

We cowered on the couch, waiting and wondering if she would pull the trigger. . . .

And then, just like that, Mom lowered the gun and began to sob: "I'm sorry! I'm sorry! Mama would never hurt you."

She curled up in a ball on the dirty floor and cried herself to sleep. We did not move right away; we stayed frozen in fear on the couch. I can't be certain what my siblings felt or were thinking as they watched our mother break into pieces before our eyes, but as for me, well, I blamed myself.

I had heard truth in her words.

Her inability to keep a man around—and the reason why—was obvious even to a little boy. Men found out she had five young children, and they ran faster than she could say all our names. And she was right—my siblings and I were constantly getting into trouble, sometimes at school, sometimes at home, but mostly with the innocent mischief of childhood. One of us was always hungry or thirsty or cold or whiny or wanting something. Little wonder that I was certain her pain was our fault.

Mom deserves a good man, but how could she find one with us in the way? I wondered.

I did not hate her for wishing we did not exist. I loved my mom. My brothers and sister loved her. And ours was true unconditional love—the kind of love people search for their entire lives. We loved Mom so much we could love her even when she did not want us, even when she thought she might prefer us dead.

That parental love so many children hold, even for parents who have hurt and disappointed them, is what the powers that be rarely understand or take into account when dealing with youngsters from troubled homes. Yet it explains a lot about the push and pull that makes it so difficult for children to break away from problem parents long enough to heal themselves.

As far as I can recall, my siblings and I never spoke about what happened that night—it was as though it had never happened. But maybe more important, *why would we tell anyone?* It never occurred to us that anyone else would believe us, much less care.

Thirty years later, I asked my older brother if he remembered the night Mom pointed the gun at us. I expected him to deny such a thing had ever happened, to call me crazy, or to ignore me altogether, so when he slowly began to describe the night just as I remembered it, I was both shocked and speechless.

I asked no more questions. I just listened.

Reliving that night from our childhood with my brother was painful, and our conversation would leave me with more questions than answers, especially as to how Mom had come to be so broken.

As my brother finished speaking, I realized one thing had not changed in the past three decades—and that was how we felt about our mom.

We both still loved her as much as we ever had.

Strength in Numbers

5 huddled together to fight off cold nights
10 eyes opened watching shadows move across the room
5 stomachs howled like wolves in search of prey
10 listening ears heard the footsteps of eight-legged creatures searching for shelter
5 vibrating organs thumped their center mass, thump, thump
4 of five mouths missed teeth that allow the song of a smile to be sung
10 hands prayed for the beatings to stop
2 of five sets of lungs struggled to exhale CO_2
10 feet seldom experienced the feel of something new
5 noses already immune to the smell of a portable medicine cabinet
10 arms endured winter months without protection

THE BOY WHO SURVIVED

5 mouths never uttered the word Daddy
10 lips never kissed a father's cheek
5 siblings sat in a circle taking turns making wishes
1 of the 5 died at the age of 12
2 of the 5 did time in prison
3 of the 5 were addicted to drugs
4 of the 5 never broke the cycle
5 of the 5 grew up bitter
5 of the 5 loved Mom to the end

Chapter 4

No Words

The judge would give my grandparents custody of my siblings and me, but first we had to return to the shelter until the paperwork could be completed. Hearing a judge tell Mom that she was unfit to be a mother had been hard enough, but watching her sob as she was dragged out of the courtroom was a horror movie come to life.

By the time my siblings and I left the courtroom, we were all wailing, and the tears continued to fall as we walked back to the shelter with our social worker.

With every step, I grew more and more agitated. By the time we reached the shelter and what would be the first bed I had ever slept in alone, I was unraveling. I threw a full-fledged temper tantrum. I cussed and screamed because I didn't have the words to describe how I felt. And as my screams turned to tears of helplessness, I decided then and there that I had to leave the shelter. I flung myself off the bed and opened the bedroom door—only to find a female member of the shelter staff on the other side.

I did my best to evade the woman, but she used her hips and legs to block my path.

"I'm leaving!" I yelled. "Get out of my way!"

"You can't leave," she said firmly. "And you need to calm down."

"Get out of my way!" I screamed.

And with that, I put both hands on her stomach and pushed. She backed up a few steps, but before I could escape, she grabbed me by my wrists and with one swift hip toss delivered me to the bedroom floor, where she promptly sat on me, pinning my arms to my sides.

What a humiliation, even for a little boy! Still, I remember her as being oddly gentle as she restrained me, doing all she could to keep me from hurting myself. Over and over again, she told me to *calm down*, but I continued to thrash about. What she couldn't know was that by physically restraining me, she had dredged up memories of abuse from my past. I was in a panic as old horrors overcame present concerns.

Twenty minutes later, exhausted and with no fight left in me, I surrendered.

With nary a word, the staffer stood, helped me up from the floor, and guided me to bed. It must have been difficult to distinguish between my sweat and my tears because my face and shirt were soaked with both. That poor shelter staffer had no idea of the flashbacks she had just put me through.

I resented her for it nonetheless.

As I lay in bed staring at the ceiling and feeling violated, she sat next to me in silence, unaware that inside I was seething with hatred. And so those first hours away from Mom passed.

The woman had done nothing wrong, and I was ashamed of what I had done. Yet I lacked the words to express how I was feeling, much less what had set me off earlier at the courthouse or later at her hand.

It had been a rough twenty-four hours for a little boy. Worse yet, I remained uncertain as to what the future held for me and my siblings.

Eventually, I fell asleep on top of the covers. I woke the next morning to a hot breakfast and the news that we would be moving to our grandparents' house later that same day.

Once our bellies were full and our few things gathered, the Carter children took their seats on yet another couch waiting for yet another social worker to pick us up. About a half an hour later, the Department of Human Services worker showed up and escorted us to her car.

Once she had us safely inside the vehicle, the DHS worker returned to the shelter. The staff members who had been taking care of us were still gathered at the front door waiting for our departure. But I couldn't help noticing that as they talked with our new social worker, she kept glancing back at the car where we waited.

I figured they were talking about us, and I wondered what was being said. The whole time, neither my siblings nor I uttered a word.

Looking back, I still have no idea what my siblings were thinking that morning as we waited in the car, but two thoughts were going through my mind: I was going to miss sleeping in a bed with clean sheets all by myself, and I was going to be sleeping on a hard floor again soon. That was about all I could deal with in the moment.

What I refused to even think about was how being placed in my grandparents' custody scared me.

I loved my grandparents but knew they did not live alone, and so as we pulled away from the shelter that day, I also knew my grandparents would not always be around to protect me from the other adults who lived in their home. Grandma cleaned a few houses that took her away from home during the day, and Grandpa had his many jobs that kept him gone both day and night. And when Grandma and Grandpa weren't home, my uncles ruled the place.

Nobody, however, had asked our opinion about any of this, including the move. When our caseworker finally did ask what we thought about moving in with our grandparents, we were already in their driveway.

"Are you excited to stay with your grandparents?" the woman asked with a smile.

We all nodded or mumbled yes because we knew that was what we were supposed to say. We lacked the where-withal to tell the social worker what living there would mean for us. She might have been feeling pleased with herself for keeping some form of a family together, but in reality, she was throwing us into a nest of vipers, most of whom we called Uncle.

To make matters worse, we also knew our grandparents did not want us living with them. They had taken us in only because they did not want anyone else to have us, and they did not want the state to split us up.

How do you tell a stranger that?

We had the answers—children almost always have seen more and know more about the threats that lurk in their home and family and school and neighborhood than grown-ups realize, and we wanted to tell somebody.

But we didn't know how or who.

We were scared.

And sadly, no one took the time to make us feel safe enough to confide in them.

Why were we so reluctant and slow to speak up?

Because we couldn't imagine that anyone existed in this world to care about us, much less help us. And we feared what would happen if we talked to anyone outside our family and then were returned back to our tribe—or, as on this day, back to the monsters who lived with my grandparents.

How do you tell a stranger about the monsters?

In truth, the fear of staying at my grandparents' house overnight, much less for a period of time, made my stomach hurt.

I felt anxious.

And I was scared.

I took a little comfort in knowing my cousins Mario and Martina had recently moved in with my grandparents too. Unfortunately, I knew they were no match for our uncles either.

Uncle Billy and Uncle David controlled two of the three bedrooms in my grandparents' house, which meant Mario, Martina, my four siblings, and I would sleep upstairs on the floor a few feet from my other uncle, Stevie.

Uncle Stevie was the last of my mother's brothers to move in with Grandma and Grandpa, so he had had to settle for the last available space, a room that would now also house us.

We did not worry about there being a monster in the closet. We had a flesh-and-blood monster sleeping on the couch right beside us.

Broken People
There are broken people everywhere
Whose hearts are cold as stones
Who no longer feel complete
And now feel alone

Our passion fades in time
Like the color in our hair
We've forgotten who we are
Now caught up in despair

Our hearts beat themselves
Replaying the battles fought
We've lost our mental strength
Our minds are tangled in thought

Time has taken its toll
Checked us off its list

Our cheeks bare the wrinkles
And scared away a kiss

Our bodies tell the story
The truth won't cost a dime
Our eyes have seen the future
Of pain frozen in time

Our days are all the same
Like knots in a rope
Today we choose to live
Our fists are full of hope

Chapter 5

Unexpected Kindness

I liked running errands for my grandma; the work made me feel useful. And since I had few friends, helping Grandma also gave me something to do—besides keeping me out of the house and away from the whims of my uncles. The only problem was my bicycle had no basket, which meant I had to improvise when carrying groceries and such.

Still, I tried to never turn down an assignment.

So when Grandma asked one day if I would go to the grocery store and bring her back a gallon of milk, I eagerly agreed. Grandma handed me a five-dollar food stamp and told me to hurry back.

I jumped on my bike and within a few minutes was at the store. A few minutes more, and I had found the milk, paid the grocer, and begun my journey back, holding the gallon of milk in my right hand and using my left to drive the bike. I knew Grandma had said to hurry, so I peddled as fast as I could.

All was going fine until, with one block to go, I hit a bump in the road. My front tire wobbled left, then right. *I was about to crash! I had to save the milk!*

I hugged the milk tighter to my chest—and did a flying dismount, trying as best I could to land on my feet and hit the ground running. I actually managed the first step and almost the second, before hitting the pavement, sliding several feet on my knees, and burning a hole in one knee of my jeans. My bike continued on, flipping several times before coming to rest.

But I was in one piece.

And so was Grandma's milk!

So, as quickly as I could muster, I dragged myself to my feet, retrieved my no longer rideable bike, and started for home—on foot.

Grandma was counting on me!

Holding the milk in one hand, I pushed the bike along with the other. As my grandparents' house came into view, my knee started to sting. I looked down—a large patch of skin was missing from the knee where my jeans had torn, lost in the slide.

I winced, but carried on to the house to complete my task. Inside, I found Grandma and delivered the milk.

Mission accomplished!

I don't remember if Grandma thanked me, but I felt good inside either way. I headed to the bathroom to see about my knee, and after washing the scrape with soap and water, returned to take my usual seat on the concrete front porch.

My knee still hurt and burned, and before long, began to throb too. When I couldn't take the pain anymore, I went looking for Grandma's aloe vera plant, one of her home remedies for burns. When I found the green plant with the pebbly, long, octopus-like arms, I pinched off a little piece from one of the leaves, returned to the front porch, and rubbed the jelly-like goo from the inside of the aloe vera leaf on my knee.

By the time I took my regular place on the floor in the living room for the night, the pain in my knee had eased enough that I soon drifted off to sleep.

Later that night, however, I was roused from sleep by a strange, fiery feeling in my knee. I figured the aloe vera salve had worn off, so I ignored the pain and tried to go back to sleep.

But the pain only got worse.

In the leftover light from Uncle Stevie in the kitchen fixing himself a late-night snack, I sat up to examine my knee. What I saw made me want to throw up: two roaches eating on my exposed flesh.

With a holler, I slapped both roaches off my sore, jumped up, and ran to the kitchen in a panic.

"What are you doing, Alton?" Uncle Stevie said.

I told him about the roaches and my sore—fully expecting him to make fun of me like usual. Instead, with an expression that never changed, he told me to go wash out my sore in the bathroom and come back to the kitchen when I'd finished.

I did as he said, and when I returned, my uncle was sitting at the kitchen table with another piece of aloe vera, a few squares of toilet paper, and some Scotch tape.

"Take a seat," he said.

Looking my knee over, again with no expression on his face, he rubbed the aloe vera on my open sore, and then covered the wound with the toilet paper and secured it on all four sides with tape.

When he finished, no words of concern or thanks were exchanged. I just excused myself from the table and returned to my spot on the living-room floor. Uncle Stevie returned to his snack.

I did not know what to think of the monster that night.

Broken Heart
Sometimes when a heart is broken
It stays that way
Why are hearts broken
It's hard for me to say
Broken hearts were made to heal
This I know for sure
It may take a little time
Love is the only cure

Hearts may grow back crooked
And never be quite the same
Change the way you see things
Don't look for who's to blame
Focus on the healing

Allow your heart to mend
The healing process hurts
But it's worth it in the end

Sometimes when a heart is broken
It's impossible to ignore
And when it finally heals
It's stronger than before

Chapter 6

White Teachers

Second grade was a hard year for me. Fresh out of my mother's custody and living with my grandparents and uncles, I was mad at the world and, if the truth be told, hated myself too. As I had expected, living on Third Street was not easy. Unable to leave my troubles at home, I too often brought them with me to school.

The morning walk to school was only a block long, too short for me to calm down from—or make sense of—whatever atrocity had happened at Grandma's the night before. I routinely arrived at school late, tired, and angry—convinced I was the only one in my class without a storybook family at home.

Thankfully, my teacher was a born educator. Every morning, she welcomed us, one by one, with a warm smile as we filed into her classroom. Mrs. Ramming did her best to reach me while I was her student. I'm sad to say that I was so broken, I never gave her much of a chance. I was like a drowning man exhausted from trying to stay afloat, too weak to cry for help or recognize it when it shows up.

But I was only a second-grader.

I am embarrassed to say that part of my hesitancy to trust Mrs. Ramming could be traced to what my family had always said about white teachers: *White teachers can't be trusted.*

That warning had been sounded loud and clear by most of the adults in my life for as long as I could remember, and as a seven-year-old, I believed it. Mrs. Ramming knew I was poor and living with my grandparents, but I am certain she had no idea what was going on inside the walls of their house only a block or so away from the school. She didn't know I was being abused and neglected—mentally, physically, and emotionally.

Mrs. Ramming could not know because I had been trained not to share *anything* about what happened at home with *anyone.*

Ever.

But I also never bothered to share anything personal of importance with her because I did not think she cared. And say she had cared, *What could she have done about it? How could she have helped me?*

At the time, I didn't know people besides your family could care about you just because you were you. I didn't know that sharing your story with a teacher could lighten the burdens you carried. *Why would I?* The only person who had ever seemed to care about me was Grandpa. But he was family. And even he didn't care enough—or couldn't find a way—to keep me safe.

What I did know for certain at the age of seven was that Mrs. Ramming disliked sending me to the office and kicking me out of her class. Even I could see that. Instead, when I misbehaved, she took to having me sit behind a big green chalkboard in the back of the classroom. The chalkboard stood about six feet tall and kept me out of sight but still able to hear the lesson.

I remember once arriving to class in such a horrible mood that neither Mrs. Ramming's sunny welcome nor any of her other efforts could improve it. My mood darkened further when her first request of the day was to get our books out so we could do a read aloud.

I was by far the worst reader in the class and so embarrassed about it that I was known to pull some crazy antics to get out of reading aloud. On this day, I refused to even get my book out despite Mrs. Ramming asking me nicely several times. Eventually, she sent me to sit alone behind the chalkboard.

My response to that request was to sweep everything on the top of my desk onto the floor and then stomp off to my new seat. But I didn't remain seated there long. After a few minutes, I got up and started to walk around.

"Alton, please sit down," said Mrs. Ramming.

I quickly did as she said. *How did she know I was out of my seat?* I wondered.

I waited a few minutes and tried again—this time doing my best to be quiet so she wouldn't hear me.

Again came the words: "Alton, please sit down."

Over the next hour, this same request was repeated many times, with me becoming more confused with each one. I could not figure out how my teacher knew when I was sitting and when I wasn't. Never did it dawn on me that Mrs. Ramming could see my legs beneath the chalkboard.

Repeatedly having to tell me to sit down, however, was impeding Mrs. Ramming's efforts to teach the rest of the class. Once more, she asked me to please remain seated and allow her to teach the lesson. I know it sounds terrible, but my response to her polite request was to start screaming and throwing whatever I could get my hands on. I became so enraged that I emerged from behind the chalkboard, pushed past my teacher, and started to overturn as many empty desks as I could get my hands on, like a little tornado.

Mrs. Ramming quietly told the other students to leave the classroom. This deprived me of my audience, which in my mind, left me with no other option but to start to curse at my teacher and rip posters off the walls. Poor Mrs. Ramming did her best to calm me down, but with every passing minute, I flew more out of control. Out of options as I was, my teacher finally did the unthinkable but only thing left: She reached out and grabbed me with both hands. Then she pulled me close and wrapped her arms around me, trapping me in a big bear hug.

The hug shocked me, and I did calm down for a moment, but then shock turned to outrage that my teacher had dared to put her hands on me. I squirmed to get free, flailing around with all my might, but Mrs. Ramming steadfastly held on, and as she did, she kept quietly telling me to *calm down.*

Calm down. Calm down. Calm down.

Eventually, I grew too tired to continue, and she was able to release me from what most children would call a bear hug but what to me had felt like the punishment of a straitjacket. Then Mrs. Ramming reached up, put her hands on my shoulders, and asked me to sit down one more time. Exhausted, I joined her on the floor. She asked what was bothering me, and though I wanted to tell her, I could not get past that she had hugged me.

Her hug was not inappropriate or meant to hurt me, and I knew that. She had held me that day because she was trying to protect me; she didn't want me to hurt myself. She had hugged me while I flopped about like a wild animal because she cared about me. Although I had never once opened up and told her about the abuse I was suffering at my grandparents', she seemed to instinctively know that something in my life was broken.

She was a *white teacher.*

And that day changed our relationship. I knew Mrs. Ramming cared about me. She would be the first of many teachers in all hues who did.

Foster Kid

My name is Alton
and I am a foster kid
It had nothing to do
with anything I did

I'm not like other kids
I don't have a dad
During parent-teacher conferences
I get sad

When Mom had a job
I watched my little brother
We all did our part
taking care of each other

My mom lost her job
so we struggled to eat
She couldn't pay rent
so we lived in the street

One day during school
I met a lady in a dress
She said, Hi, Alton,
I'm from DHS

She asked me questions
then gave me a snack
Then gave me a hug
and said she'd be back

Mom walked us to school
the very next day
We met the nice lady
who had something to say

Mrs. Carter, we know
that your life is rough
But your best right now
isn't good enough

My mom got sad
and started to cry
She had to give us up
and told us goodbye

The nice lady took us
to a house down the street
There lived a couple
named Alice and Pete

A yard with a fence
and the house painted red
Best part of it all
I had my own bed

There's food on the table
and shoes on my feet
I attend the same school
that's just down the street

The lady in the dress
left me and my brother
She had to leave
and go check on our mother

We are foster kids now
until Mom gets us back
She is working real hard
to get back on track

Chapter 7

Crybaby

I was a crybaby, and everybody made sure I knew it. For whatever reason, as a little boy, my first reaction to almost anything that happened was to cry—and I did so without hesitation and with gusto. Not too long ago, I had a chance to ask my cousin Martina, one of the cousins who had lived with us at Grandma's back in the day, about this.

"What do you remember about me when I was little?" I asked.

The first words out of her mouth, I kid you not, were, "Alton, you know you were the biggest baby in the family, and you were afraid of everything."

She remembered me as a tattletale too—telling on people so often that my siblings and cousins kept all sorts of things from me, I would later learn.

"I remember that anytime someone tried to fight you, you'd fall down on your back and kick *at them*," she said. (You notice she didn't say kick *them*.)

My memory of that time—living under the same roof on Third Street with my grandparents, three uncles, two cousins, and four siblings—is an orchestrated effort by everyone, young or old, to make me tough.

That meant being told constantly that I was weak and that men don't cry. My many siblings and cousins picked fights with me with the sole objective of making me *tough*, or so they said. All I remember of those fights is being beat up or humiliated. Every once in a while, I tried to fight back, but the ending was always the same— me in tears. No matter whom I was fighting.

I remember one fight with Martina that began with us screaming and yelling at each other—my cousin on one end of the living room, me on the other. Suddenly, without warning, Martina rushed me, landing me on my back. This would have embarrassed most boys, but as my cousin has already pointed out, on my back with my feet in the air was my normal fight position.

I remember drawing my knees to my chest and kicking wildly while Martina stood over me screaming, "You got beat up by a girl! Get up, you big baby, and fight me!"

I yelled back, but with much less confidence, it must be said: "Martina, I will get up and kick your butt!"

Martina, to her credit, did actually back up a few feet to allow me to do just that. Thinking it was safe, I rolled over on my side only to see Martina grab a wooden tennis racket. That brought me to my feet fast, and I assumed my fight position. I had no intention of hitting Martina; I was just hoping she would put the racket down and call a truce.

Instead, she grabbed the handle with both hands and pointed the tennis racket at my face like a loaded gun. We both knew she didn't need a tennis racket to defeat me. Nonetheless, I yelled once more that not only was I no longer scared of her, but I was also tired of her picking on me.

Martina took two steps forward, and I threw a hard right, hoping to hit her square in the face. I knew hitting girls—even bullies or angry cousins—was always wrong, but Carter family rules, misguided as they might be, said I had to respond. I watched as my fist extended in slow motion, only to have Martina save me from myself. She drew the tennis racket back and swung down hard, striking my right hand between the first and second knuckles.

Crack—I heard as the racket and my hand made contact. I jerked my hand back. It had already started to swell, and then it started to hurt. The pain seemed to increase with each second that passed.

One second. Two seconds.

On the third, I fell to the floor crying.

Yet all and all, except for my injured hand, the fight had been pretty typical for us, only this time, instead of gloating, as she normally would have, Martina threw the racket to the floor and ran out the door.

I went downstairs to find Grandma so I could tell her what Martina had done. I found my grandma sitting on the edge of her bed.

I gave her a report on what had just happened. When I finished my very detailed story, I stuck out the injured hand so she could see the damage for herself.

Grandma looked my hand over and declared it broken. Off we went to the doctor, and a few hours later, I returned home with my hand in a cast. I promptly went around showing off the cast to everyone—everyone that is except my cousin Martina.

Martina was nowhere to be found!

That night as we all got ready to go to bed, Martina finally slipped in without a word, changed into her pajamas, and took her spot on the blankets on the floor.

Once she had settled in, I tried to show her my cast—even though I expected her to react by making fun of me or calling me names, or pouncing on the chance to tell me how the whole thing was all my fault.

Instead, my cousin started to cry and apologize.

I was flabbergasted! Until that moment, no one had ever apologized to me for anything—no matter what they had done, no matter how badly they might have hurt me. Having Martina, of all people, apologize to me made me feel almost human for the first time.

In my life, I had always found it easier to assume every misfortune that came my way was all my fault—if only because I was usually the one who ended up being blamed for whatever happened. So naturally, on this day, I had just assumed once again that I had done something to deserve my hand being broken.

After her apology, Martina hugged me, saying, "You know I love you—don't you, Alton?"

No, I thought, *no, I didn't.*

I truly had no idea that any of my cousins even liked me, much less loved me. But I kept that kernel of information to myself.

I wasn't about to ruin a moment I was to remember the rest of my life.

Two Sides to Every Story
There are two sides to every story
And both are very real
I see the conflict that exists
Between what I think and how I feel

It's hard to pick a side
They seem so far apart
12 inches is the distance
Between my brain and my heart

A simple state of conflict
Exists between the two
Neither side agrees
I don't know what to do

My mind is plotting the future
My heart remembers the past
My thoughts are constantly racing
My heart can't move that fast

Chapter 8

Stick Soldiers

When I was a little boy, if we ever got a toy to play with, it never lasted long. Toys were quickly either lost or played with so hard that they fell apart. With little or no money for the necessities of life, our family had no money for luxuries, toys being one of them.

So we had to find other ways to entertain ourselves—and that usually involved either a makeshift ball of some kind or a stick. Or someone else's ball or bat. We played football and basketball with neighborhood kids in the park, and one of our favorite games was a good game of hide-and-seek. But one of my all-time favorite games was playing toy soldiers with my younger brother, Watell.

We never had actual green plastic soldiers like you get at the store; instead, we created soldiers out of sticks we found in the yard or park.

One army would be made from sticks that had been broken into two-inch lengths. The other, composed of sticks pulled from the willow tree out in front of the house. Those were also broken into pieces, but we left a few leaves on these sticks so we could tell the difference between the two armies.

Once we had enough sticks for two armies, we went looking for a battlefield.

Now we would not have turned down an army of plastic soldiers from the store if someone had thought to give us such a gift, but we didn't mind our stick soldiers either. The great thing about using sticks for soldiers is that you don't need flat ground to stand up the men. We simply pushed the sticks into the ground, and our soldiers stood there as long as we had need.

Once in place, our stick soldiers were like chess pieces. We would each choose a stick, pull it out of the ground, and move it to the center of the battlefield, where the two stick soldiers would face off. The actual combat usually consisted of us holding the bottom of our respective soldier and running the soldiers into each other.

There was never a clear way to determine who had won the battle, much less the war. So instead, when our arms got tired, we would just agree to declare one of the soldiers the winner. The stick that lost the fight was given to the other team to be held as a prisoner. We did our best to keep the game even and took turns handing over sticks until finally, we each had only one stick soldier.

Every once in a while, we would change the game up— separating the two armies by, say, making a river through the middle of the battlefield. Whenever we played stick soldiers with a river, the defeated sticks were placed in the river to float until the next game.

Looking back on such childhood games, I realize that we might have been poor in material things, but we were rich with imagination and creativity—we saw in a stick something no one else might have seen.

Being bored was never a problem in the Carter tribe. We always found ways to pass the time, although the lack of guidance from the adults in our family meant our choices were not always safe or legal.

But those are stories for another time.

I prefer to remember the innocent times, the good times—and how playing with something like stick soldiers showed how resourceful we could be.

The Past
It's all about the past
and the past is all you got
Your past is full of wounds
and it hurts like you've been shot
Your dreams contain memories
and moments you never had
Your dreams are broken and empty
and your dreams are mostly sad
So if your dreams are painful
and they take away your voice
Create the dreams you hope for
and remember you have a choice

Chapter 9

Doghouse Blues

Sometimes on the weekend, the families in our neighborhood were known to gather for a game of touch football in the park across the street from my grandparents' house. I was lucky enough to get to play, but that doesn't mean I ever got to touch the football.

And that was okay with me.

I was just happy to be included.

The adults picked the teams and chose the quarterbacks too. They always made sure everyone played—no matter the age, size, or gender—but they only threw the ball to the older kids and adults. That never stopped me from letting everyone know when I was open for a pass even if it usually came to naught—save for one magical day.

Ted and Danny—two adults who regularly played football with us—were declared captains for the game.

ALTON CARTER

I had played ball with both of them before but ended up on Ted's team that day. As was my way, every single time we were on offense, I ran down the field screaming, "I'm open" or "Throw it to me!"—raising my arms high in the air in hopes that Ted would see me.

Despite all this, I never actually expected him to throw the ball to me because he never had before, not once. Yet on this special day, before this game was over, the impossible had happened not *once* but *twice*!

And Ted had become my new hero.

We lost that game, but I had gained a new friend.

Afterward, I followed Ted home. He lived right around the block from the park. We hadn't gone far when he reached into his back pocket and pulled out a small round can. He pried off the lid and then reached in the shallow container with two fingers and took a pinch of the loose brown contents, placing the leaves under his bottom lip.

The only people I had ever seen dip were baseball players on TV. Most of them seemed cool; Ted seemed cool. I wanted to be cool. So when he went to put the lid back on the can, I stopped him and asked for a dip.

"Have you ever dipped before?" he asked.

"Oh, yes!" I quickly replied. "I do it all the time with my brother." That was a lie, but I wanted my new older friend to think I was cool, so I told myself that made the lie okay.

Ted looked doubtful but he handed over the can, and then I repeated the same sequence I had just watched him go through, opening the tin, pinching the tobacco leaves, and placing the tobacco under my bottom lip.

58

The only problem was I did not get all of the dip in the right place the first try, so I spent the next few minutes spitting the excess on the ground as Ted watched with a funny look on his face. When I handed the can back to him, Ted looked at me closely and asked, "Alton, are you sure you've dipped before?"

Again, I lied, assuring Ted that I had taken a dip just yesterday. Ted still looked doubtful. "Be sure not to swallow the dip or any spit," he said with a concerned look.

Still aiming to impress, I told him I knew that, and we continued to walk. Determined not to look like an amateur dipper in front of my new older friend, I continued to mimic whatever Ted did. If Ted spit, I spit. If Ted took another dip, I took another dip.

We soon reached his house, and Ted said he needed to work on his fence and asked me to help. I followed him around back; Ted ducked into a shed and reappeared with pliers and wire in hand.

"What are you doing to your fence?" I asked.

"I have some holes to close so my dog doesn't get out," Ted said.

I looked around the yard. I saw no dog but did spot a small A-frame doghouse under a tree by the house.

"He's inside," Ted said with a little nod toward the house. With that settled, Ted began to work his way down the fence, looking for holes that he quickly fixed and making sure the fencing was firmly attached to each of the posts.

As we worked our way around the enclosure, however, I began to feel queasy.

Oh, no! I thought. *I've been swallowing my spit!*

I did not dare tell Ted this—that would only have blown my image as an experienced dipper. So I tried to look normal, while I fought off the sick feeling welling up in my belly.

More time passed. By then, I was not only sick to my stomach but also beginning to feel dizzy and awful hot. Thinking it might be wise to get out of the heat of the sun, I made my way over to a tree near the house and crawled up on top of the doghouse. With every passing minute, I felt worse and the urge to lie down somewhere grew stronger, until finally I was lying flat on my back on the doghouse roof.

By this time, Ted had noticed something was up and walked over to ask again if I was okay.

I assured him I was fine.

He clearly did not believe me.

"Did you swallow some spit, Alton?" he said.

I felt too rotten to lie again, and so confessed that I had forgotten and swallowed some dip, but quickly assured him I would be okay.

Ted walked away, shaking his head in disbelief and went back to working on the fence. He hadn't hammered his first nail when I started to puke.

Unable to stand because the backyard was now spinning, I tried lifting my head, which only made me want to barf. I rolled onto my side to keep from puking on myself. I was so dizzy and sick by then that I couldn't locate Ted nor could I holler for help. Thankfully, Ted appeared at my side with a glass of water. He told me to drink it. Then, looking disappointed, he said that as soon as I was able, I needed to go home and lie down.

"Could I stay here a few more minutes? I promise I'll go home just as soon as I can," I said.

Ted nodded and headed inside, leaving me all alone in the heat on the doghouse.

When I could finally stand, I stumbled out of Ted's backyard and down the street to my grandparents' house. I struggled up the front steps into the living room and onto the couch, where I promptly fell asleep.

No one had missed me.

No one was there to take care of me.

But then, no one was around to tell me to get off the couch and go sleep on the floor where I belonged, either.

So on the couch, I remained.

Later that night, I woke up thirsty, with a headache so bad that I felt as if my head might explode. I was still on the couch but still a little queasy too. Wondering if I would ever feel good again, I vowed never to dip again.

I Know Me

I know exactly who I am
I'm aware of what I've done
I'm broken in some places
Am I the only one?

My prayers are often selfish
My faith is par at best
I hope there's room for me
I'm not sure I'd pass the test

My past is full of pain
So now I act real tough
Moments I gave my best
But is my best enough?

Is there a place in heaven
Or a chance that I may go?
If I'm judged by the rest
It's hard for me to know

I'm flawed and partially damaged
I'm somewhat insecure
Christ came to save us all
But for me I'm not so sure.

Chapter 10

The Carter Tribe

Scientists consider a sense of belonging to be a basic human need, as vital as the need for food and shelter. *Feeling like you belong* is critical for a person to see the value in life. For most people, the first place they find that *feeling of belonging* is with their family.

I know that was true for me.

When it came to my family, my desire—and the desire of my siblings, cousins, uncles, and even grandparents—to be part of the Carter tribe was strong, often stronger than common sense.

Our family was a dysfunctional mess and fiercely loyal to one another—and we proved our loyalty by standing together at all cost. What happened inside the walls of the Carter house stayed in the Carter house, regardless of how bad we hurt one another physically or emotionally.

I am certain one of the reasons Grandpa tended to leave home during physical altercations between his sons or his sons and grandchildren, instead of intervening and calling the police, was because of that same blind loyalty.

Grandpa Carter might have wanted to call the police for help or to report what he had seen or what had happened, but he never once did. He might have been different from the rest of the family in so many positive ways—from his ability to function in the world to his ability to command respect at work, but his desire to be part of the Carter tribe trumped everything else at home.

That was clear even to his own grandchildren.

Looking back, it seems almost unbelievable not only how my grandparents refused to get involved in the fights and but also how my aunts and uncles turned a blind eye whenever their siblings beat their children. There was not a person of conscience among the lot, not one who would speak up if someone else crossed a line. Not even when their children or grandchildren were left unattended for days or went hungry or had no hot water to take a bath or no clean clothes to wear to school.

In the Carter tribe, you could raise your children however you saw fit, and no one would interfere or say a thing about it—good or bad.

Other rules of the tribe went unsaid but nonetheless were enforced: Men were supposed to be tough and show no sign of weakness. Crying was unacceptable and not to be tolerated. Men were expected to defend themselves against anyone who challenged them, no matter how silly or petty the reason—and under no circumstance were you ever to let anyone outside the family disrespect you or talk bad about your tribe or any other member of the tribe. If anybody did so, you were expected to fight them and *make them eat their words.*

The women in our family were also tough, and all had the scars to prove that they adhered to the same Carter tribal rules as the men with one exception: During the time I belonged to the tribe, I never saw Grandpa lay a hand on Grandma. I did, however, see her hit him and throw things at him. This was confusing to me—seeing her hurt the only man in the family who did anything to keep us all housed and fed, the only man who never wanted to hurt anybody.

Equally mind-boggling was how every woman in my family managed to find herself in a relationship with a man who hurt her—every single one except Grandma.

All the women in the Carter tribe had multiple children by different men—except Grandma. And all of their children had little or no contact with their fathers—again except Grandma's. My mother, aunt, and cousins were all beautiful, but the misguided traditions of our tribe, combined with how poorly they thought of themselves, seemed to lead them to settle for men who always seemed to bring out the worst in them, not the best.

To a one, the Carters believed the world had forgotten us and left us behind like a tribe of castaways. But at times, it also felt as though the adults in our tribe had passed down a victim mentality like it was genetic. We were great at making excuses, excuses for being poor, excuses for being out of work, excuses for being unable to pay the bills, excuses for hitting the kids, excuses for drinking too much. Yet even as a child, I could see that most of this had nothing to do with the color of our skin and everything to do with the choices made.

As a family, we seized every opportunity to blame society for the way we had turned out. Our inability to hold down or get a job was never from our not having a high school diploma or the necessary training or skills or resume but because all employers were racist.

We all had dreams—even Uncle Stevie, I suspect.

But the first reflex of our tribe—should any member of the family dare to try to be more—was to belittle or disparage that child or sibling or cousin for daring to even dare aspire to a better life, to a life different than the Carter tribe norm.

We lived by one and only one expectation: *Protect the tribe at all cost.*

We learned by example to sacrifice ourselves for the tribe. If one of our dreams was to be anything else but part of the tribe, the others would do all they could to sabotage that dream—or they would spout negativity to the dreamer until he sabotaged himself and fell back into his proper place in the tribe. The words *that's where you belong* were never said, but you heard them loud and clear.

As for the children in the Carter tribe, we all knew we were seen as more of a burden than a blessing. Our elders would say we were loved, but their actions belied that. And every single one of us children saw things that would damage us for life.

With so little supervision, we spent a lot of time fending for ourselves like a den of wolf pups. In the wild, any wolf pup less aggressive than his or her brothers and sisters gets less food. If pups are too persistent in begging for food, adult wolves will growl to hush them. Adult wolves are even known to leave the den to avoid their pups. Sound familiar?

But the Carter tribe went the wolf pack one better. At an early age, we learned to steal—not only to feed ourselves but for entertainment. We were forced to drink alcohol and smoke marijuana as grade-schoolers. Before we could walk, we became so immune to the sight of adults hitting each other that we thought that was how all disagreements were solved.

Trained to keep secrets, we all basically took a family oath to never trust white people, teachers, DHS workers, neighbors, and the law. As children, we learned fathers fell into this same category of people never to trust or seek out. For a Carter, a father was a scary imaginary being like a snow monster, a monster never seen, while a single mother raising multiple children on her own, with no child support, was the norm.

Carter children entered school with undiagnosed learning disabilities, and most of us dropped out before finishing ninth grade, just as generations of Carters before us had. Worse yet, we bought into the hypocrisy of the Carter tribe—and its crazy logic about how to live life:

You don't need to get to school on time. Or pay attention or work hard when there.

*You don't need a diploma or a college de-
gree to get ahead in this world—much less an
advanced degree.*

*You don't need to learn to read—much
less learn to read well.*

You don't need a job. Or skills.

You don't need to learn how to parent.

You don't need to be honest. Or fair.

Or kind. Or generous. Or helpful.

Or lawful. Or a good citizen. . . .

Or educated.

That last one still leaves me dumbfounded.

Where did such an idea come from? For generations,
most Americans have agreed on one thing: The best way
to ensure that your children have a good life—a life with
better choices than you or previous generations had—is
to give those children the best education possible.

But in my family, it was as if the Carter tribe lived in
an upside-down world where good was bad and bad was
good. And because no one read us bedtime stories or fairy
tales and because we didn't pay attention to the teacher at
school, we rarely heard that a different way existed.

And so nothing improved. No matter our age, no matter how much the Carter tribe's code of life hurt us or
those around us, no matter if every single norm of society
made it clear how horribly, horribly wrong the Carter
beliefs were—we toed the line. We all toed the line.

Even me.

Until I was nine years old. . . .

. . . until the night I walked away from my tribe.

. . . until the night Uncle Stevie threw me down a flight of stairs for refusing to drink his whiskey, and that violent act became one too many for me.

On that night, my uncle followed me down the stairs so he could deliver several more kicks as I laid crumpled on the floor—his way of telling me that I was always to do whatever he told me to do.

I, however, for the first time refused to adhere to his rules and mustered enough strength to run to the phone and call 9-1-1.

The police came, arrested Uncle Stevie, and with no fuss, took him off to jail as they are supposed to do. But there was no happy ending.

I had broken the first rule of the tribe.

Grandma made that clear.

So I banished myself from the tribe.

I slept in the park that night, believing I was the shallow root in the big family tree.

I couldn't go back to Grandma's either because I knew as soon as she could get the money together for bail, Grandma would go and get Uncle Stevie out of jail, never giving a minute's thought as to how ludicrous it was that her grade-school-aged grandchildren knew about such a thing as bail. And once my uncle returned, I also knew he would mete out his revenge on me.

Better for me to go.

For years, I thought my family turned their backs on me that night because in my eyes, they had all the power. What I realize now is that I was the one who turned my back on them, on their way of life, on their fear, on their hate, on the poor choices they had made and kept making.

I was only a grade-schooler.

But I saw my departure as an act of pure survival. Still for years to come, my heart would ache for my family and for their love and acceptance, even as that night opened my young eyes to the misguided ways of the Carter tribe.

Going forward, I coped by telling myself they had never loved me in the first place. Yet I would also continue to seek their approval—always wondering what I had to do to win a word of praise or admiration from my mother or my grandmother or my brothers and sisters or cousins.

I became the first person in my family to graduate from high school, the first person to go to college, the first to earn a college degree.

I became a policeman, a husband, a father, a coach, a businessman, a youth minister, and an author.

I thought at least one of those achievements would make my family to see how wrong they were about me.

Instead, my achievements separated us more.

I hoped my personal successes would make them proud of me. In reality, my ability to hold down a job and make ends meet brought my former tribe running to me for handouts. Whenever I dared refuse, I was called a sellout and told I didn't care about my family.

At times, my desire to be back in the tribe made me do things that defied logic—and put me and later my own family at risk. The truth is that no matter how hard I tried or how much I gave, I would never have the price of admission to the Carter tribe again. I would be alone, at least at first and for the rest of my childhood.

And I had to learn to live with that.

My mother's death in 2013 brought all this home again as nothing ever had before. I realized that all I had ever wanted was her approval, for her to be proud of me, proud to have me as her son.

We had been distant for many years by then. And as desperately as I still sought her approval, what she actually felt for me, until the moment that she left this earth, was only resentment. She resented me because she couldn't take credit for the man I had become.

Now she was gone.

It took time, but I came to realize that only forgiveness could fill the hole she had left behind. And I committed to forgiving her—and myself.

That meant letting go of how things were between us when she died and what we had suffered as an estranged mother and son. And, so I did. I chose to let go, so I could go forward, believing that deep down, even if she never said it or told me, she was proud to have me as her son.

As for my siblings' dislike for me, I believe now that was not because I left them. I am convinced it is because they did not go with me.

I Decide
I'm not who you say I am
I'm stronger than you know
You will not decide my fate
or decide how far I will go

You may hurt my feelings
on occasion make me cry
You will not break my spirit
no matter how hard you try

I'm strong and courageous
even if you don't believe
You set up stumbling blocks
and still I will achieve

Today I am different
than I was before
I am fragile on the surface
and tough at my core

I hate that you see me
as less than a man
If you knock me down
tomorrow, still I will stand

Chapter 11

I Want To Be Like Grandpa

I am told my grandfather is the one who named me, giving me the name of the gentleman who had given him his first job when he moved to Oklahoma. Alton was an unusual name, but everyone called me Alton—everyone, that is, but Grandpa, who called me Al.

I don't know whether he ever knew it or not, but I loved hearing him call me that. It was like we shared something special just the two of us.

Whenever Grandpa was around, I was his little shadow, morning, noon, and night. I would get up early to watch him get ready for work, a routine that started the night before with him preparing his clothes the way his father had always done.

His routine began with Grandpa taking his dress pants by the bottom cuffs, giving the pants a good shake, and then laying them down on top of the bed. He then would run his hand over the pants, pressing down to make sure the material was flat, smooth, with seams lined up evenly. Next, he would lift the mattress and lay the pants on top of the box spring, about six inches from the edge.

Once he had his pants in the perfect position, he placed a towel over them before laying the mattress back down. Done correctly, sleeping on your clothes like this will smooth and crease them just like an iron, Grandpa liked to say. And you don't need electricity—nor an iron or even an ironing board—to do it.

One of my other favorite things to do was to watch Grandpa shave, one of the rare times I got him all to my-self. He made the funniest faces while shaving, especially when he shaved under his nose.

With each stroke of the razor, I would inch closer and closer, until I was so close Grandpa would have to stop and ask me to please give him a little room. I'd scoot back some on the toilet lid where I liked to stand for a better view, and our little routine would start all over again.

When Grandpa was done, he'd splash his face with water and then dry off with a towel. Not once did I ever see him notice the dirty bathroom sink, yet he never failed to look at me after shaving and ask, "Did I miss a spot, Al?"

"Nope, you sure didn't," I always answered.

This was his cue to finish off his shave with a good dollop of Old Spice After Shave lotion. Shaving done, he returned to the bedroom, retrieved his clothes from under the mattress, and dressed for the day. Then it was on to a stop in the kitchen for his morning cup of coffee and, if he had time, a bowl of cornflakes. Most mornings, the latter required that he pick roaches out of his cereal bowl before adding the milk, something else he never commented on or seemed to notice.

Although my grandpa was a good and reliable worker, he rarely made it to work on time because he always insisted on stopping and helping anyone who was having car trouble that he came across along the way there.

Once I asked him, "Why do you always stop?"

His reply has stayed with me: "First, Al, it's the right thing to do, and second, you never know when you will need help from someone someday."

Grandpa might have been treated poorly at home, but away from home, he was valued as a good man of high integrity. Even as a child when I visited him at his job on campus, where he was a manager, I could tell that his employees liked him and looked up to him. I think that's partly because Grandpa was never too busy to stop what he was doing and help one of his employees. Although he was the boss, Grandpa could often be found mopping floors and taking out the trash—he led by example and treated everyone with respect. And his staff respected him too, and I could tell that mattered to him.

Basically, Grandpa lived by the Golden Rule:

> *Do onto others as you would have them*
> *do unto you.*

If only that rule could have been a rule at home! I was proud that so many people respected and listened to my grandpa at work and sporting events, but I was heartbroken that his own children and other grandchildren didn't seem to see him in the same way.

I know we often embarrassed him and caused him grief, but not once did he show it or let our failings compromise who he was—at least outside the home. I believe he would have done the same at home if Grandma had let him.

I don't know how many people in our family knew it, but Grandpa had an interesting past of his own that he rarely shared. I only learned about it by happenstance. When I lived with my grandparents, Grandpa's second job was refereeing, and riding once with him to a football game, I got the courage to ask where he had grown up.

Grandpa said he had been born in Stillwater, a town on the plains of Oklahoma, and had lived there with his parents while in grade school. He said his parents spent more time fighting than they did getting along, and by the time he was thirteen, he was tired of it and packed a bag and left home.

"Did you ever go back?" I asked.

"Not until I was an adult," he said.

"How did you survive?"

My grandfather heaved a big sigh and replied, "I got a job picking cotton for a nickel a day."

The pay sustained him, and then one day, instead of giving him five cents for his day of work, the landowner gave him a quarter—Grandpa had been that much more productive than the man's other workers. I guffawed at his reward, but Grandpa stopped me.

"You laugh, Al, but twenty-five cents was a lot of money back then."

While I had a hard time believing a quarter was ever a lot of money for a day's work, I could tell the landowner's sense of fairness had made a lasting impression on my grandpa. As we rode along, Grandpa said he had learned something from every job he ever had—good jobs and bad ones. The lessons he'd learned ran the gamut—some being good, as with the cotton bonus for being extra productive; others, less so, but all valuable.

What could you learn from a bad job? I wondered.

Maybe sensing my confusion, Grandpa launched into a story from his days working at an Oklahoma bowling alley. Still a teenager at the time, he spent his time setting pins for the bowlers. Many a time, Grandpa said, he had to reset pins for people who behaved like jerks.

"What do you mean *jerks?*" I asked.

"They would roll the bowling ball down the lane before I was out of the way," Grandpa said.

"Did you ever give one of them a piece of your mind?"

Grandpa shook his head. "If I had cussed them out or yelled at them, I would have lost my job. Then where would I be?" He drove a ways before speaking again. "One of the greatest teaching moments a person can have is watching someone else make a mistake, then you know what not to do."

I must have again looked puzzled again because he added, "Al, look at your uncles. They are constantly mistreating people and cheating people. And look at where that has gotten them."

Grandpa went on to explain that he had not ignored the taunting from the bowlers because he was weak but because he was strong enough to control himself, even as a young boy. He believed the experience at the bowling alley had made him a better person, a better man.

Instead of getting upset back then, Grandpa said, he had learned to work faster so no one could hit him with the ball. He worked so hard and so quickly that the manager put him in charge of two lanes while everyone else worked one—more work for doing a good job. Some people would have thought that unfair. My grandpa, however, saw it as learning how to work better and more efficiently, how to make yourself valued and indispensable at work. After several more jobs over the next few years, Grandpa said he joined the military.

He fell silent then.

I sat quiet, not knowing why.

And then, as abruptly, Grandpa spoke again.

"Al, everybody has had bad things happen to them. Some use their past to motivate them, and some are stuck in the past feeling sorry for themselves."

Grandpa pulled the truck over onto the side of the road and stopped. Then he told me to look at him: "Al, don't you ever let anyone feel sorry for you," he said. "You would also do yourself good not to ever feel sorry for yourself either."

He paused and then asked, "Do you hear me?"

"Yes!" I said.

Grandpa checked the rearview mirror. A few cars passed by, and then he eased the truck back into traffic and continued down the road. I could tell he was done talking, so I kept quiet the rest of the trip.

We would go on to have these little talks every now and then through the years, and I treasure all of them. I suspect a good part of who I am can be traced to what I learned in those conversations with my grandpa. I knew I was lucky to have a grandpa who would talk to me about such matters—not like I was a little boy, but like someone who was ready to learn about how the world worked and what would be needed to make your way in it.

Grandpa's talks weren't always about work, and I will never forget the day that working in the yard with him turned into a lesson about love.

As we pulled weeds side by side, I suddenly declared: "I love you more than I do anyone else in our family!"

Grandpa stopped and asked me to repeat myself.

"I love you more than anyone else in the family."

He looked at me blankly.

Thinking maybe Grandpa wanted to know why I loved him most, I volunteered that I loved him the most because he did not treat me like everyone else did.

Grandpa shook his head. And then, with a frustrated look on his face, he replied, "Al, love doesn't work that way. You either love someone or you don't. There are no degrees in love. There are different types of love, say a mother's love for her children or a husband's love for his wife, but love is love. Don't ever say you love someone more than someone else. Your Grandma and I have been through some very hard times, but through it all, we never stopped loving each other."

I can still recall, in the aftermath of those words from the man I respected most in the world, trying to convince myself that I loved Uncle Stevie and my mom as much as I loved Grandpa, but I just couldn't do it. I could not reconcile my feelings for my family with how they treated me and one another.

All these years later, I still don't understand why my grandfather put up with the fighting, with the drugs and alcohol, with the sloth and profanity in his house.

None of that was him.

None of that was his way.

In every way that matters, Grandpa was the complete opposite of every other person in our family. He got up every morning intending to be better and do better by others and by himself.

Every Carter who lived in his home was in the presence of a man who had overcome, a man whom they could have learned from. But they were all so blinded with self-pity, they could not see Thomas L. Carter for who he was, much less all he did for them every single day.

I know that had to pain Grandpa.

And it fills me with regret for what could have been.

Too Late
What if you waited too late
What if you've become what you hate
What if your depression has become your obsession
What if your fear is now your love
What if your hug is now a shove

THE BOY WHO SURVIVED

What if your anger has made you a stranger
What if the past stole your joy until it's only a broken toy
What if your confusion is now an illusion
What if your thoughts lost their way
So now your voice has nothing to say
What if your heart has been torn apart
What if you waited too late
What if you've become what you hate

Chapter 12

A Mother's Gift to Her Son

There is something special about the bond formed between a mother and her son, a connection I have always
found difficult to put into words.

The way I imagine the relationship, every time a child
looks up at his mother, he sees an angel looking back
at him. Before he can speak, he knows his mother loves
him. In his mom's arms, he feels protected, safe from any
harm that might come his way.

And that makes sense to me.

Her belly was his first home. And after his birth, his
mom fed him, changed his dirty diapers, and took care of
him when he was sick or scared or hurt.

I believe besides love, the greatest gift a mother can
give her child is memories. I have many memories from
my life, but I didn't know how different they were from

those of other kids' until I became much older. And to this day, I tell myself that the best memories my mother and I shared must have been before I could remember.

I tell myself that my mother loved me, gave birth to me, and must have taken care of me while I was a baby. I can't remember any of this, of course, but I assume that when I was young, she did all the things a mother is supposed to do for her child.

I do know that I longed for her attention as I grew older, but I don't remember ever getting it. I would play in front of her so she could see me use my imagination. I would share my art from school with her, hoping that she would be impressed.

I don't recall any of that drawing even a small smile.

I do know now that it isn't normal for a mom to watch her child play through an empty pill bottle. I do know now that there is something wrong when a mom looks past a child's artwork to the outfit she plans to wear that night. And I do know the pain of her absence even when she was so close I could have touched her.

How many other times did I have a bad dream and run to her, but she wasn't in her room? How many times did I need something to eat and run to the kitchen only to find nothing to stop the pain in my belly? How many times did I fall and scrape my knee and run to her to kiss it and make it better only to find her in the bedroom waiting on some stranger hand and foot?

Too many times to count is what my memory recalls.

Yet whenever I made a mistake or did something wrong, she certainly seemed to see me. At those times,

I got beatings with belts, hangers, extension cords, and branches—never words nor consequences to help me do better the next time.

A mother's gift to her son should be memories that make him appreciate life, his family, and her. My memories of being a child should be filled with stories of Mom coming to the rescue and Mom hugging me when I did something well or cool.

I should have memories of my mom rocking me to sleep, reading me a bedtime story, saying my prayers, kissing me good night, and wishing me sweet dreams.

Instead, I have nightmares that haunt me to this day.

I was afraid of my mom because her touching me was not the way a mother should ever touch her son. Her affection made me hate every inch of my body. Her house was never a safe place because there was no room that could protect me from the gift she gave me, a gift saturated in betrayal, lies, neglect, and emptiness.

But that is what my mother gave to her son.

That is the memory she left me.

Chapter 13

The Secret to Happy

Growing up in complete chaos, I could easily allow the unfortunate times to take up most of my memory real estate. I am a survivor, but that doesn't mean I have forgotten all the bad things that happened to me along the way.

What I have done is learn not to let those bad times drown out the good times. And I have mastered holding tight to the good memories from my childhood, as rare as they might be.

That is the secret to being happy.

And there were good times. Every once in a while, Mom would rise to the challenge that came with raising five children on her own. Yes, such moments were few and far between, and maybe that is what made them so special then—to this day.

Seeing my mother smile could chase away hunger pangs and brighten a house without electricity. As children, we vied to make her smile. And we memorized what could. A family dinner with enough food on the table for all of us could make her smile. But Mom never smiled brighter than when a new stranger came to live with us. I hated every man that ever moved into our little house, but I tolerated them because seeing Mom smile was worth whatever abuse they would dish out to me and my siblings or even to Mom.

The upside to having a stranger play Daddy was that for awhile, Mom transformed into a mother anyone would be happy to have.

The presence of those strangers motivated Mom to clean the house and to make dinner. Convinced that each stranger might be Mr. Right, Mom would stop taking the pink pills cold turkey. She would welcome us at the door when we returned from school. Full of life and energy, she would wash our clothes in the bathtub and hang them on the clothesline so we had clean clothes for school. She would paint my sister's fingernails, comb and braid her hair, and even seem to enjoy doing it. At bedtime, Mom would join us on the floor and either sing us to sleep or put on her favorite Smokey Robinson record and listen with us until we fell asleep.

When my mom was happy, she would help us get dressed, fix us breakfast, and even walk us to school. The special twinkle in Mom's eye at such times was so engaging that seeing it could almost chase away the memories of how we usually lived. Her happiness was contagious:

We even behaved better in school because the last thing we wanted was to destroy the fairy tale.

Unfortunately, by the time I was eight years old, I knew how the fairy tale always ended. I knew that eventually the fighting with the stranger would begin, and then the stranger would disappear. Until that day of reckoning came, however, the fairy tale could provide moments that made us feel like a big, normal, happy family.

I will always remember the stranger who took us to the local drive-in like a big, happy family. Mom made baloney sandwiches and loaded them and a six-pack of grape pop, along with a couple of blankets, into the back seat of the stranger's car. We all piled in and headed to the east side of town. Several blocks away from the drive-in, Mom told us to get down on the floor of the car, and then she covered us with the blankets. She told us to be quiet and not to move.

We thought Mom was playing a game and began to wiggle and giggle. Mom shushed us, saying if we couldn't be still she would have the stranger turn the car around and go home.

That silenced us.

We went motionless under the blankets as the stranger pulled into the drive-in entrance. I felt the car slow to a stop and then heard the stranger roll down the driver's window. "Good evening sir, just two tickets tonight?" a voice asked.

The stranger replied, "Yes, two tickets."

There were sounds of money changing hands, and then the voice said, "Enjoy the movie."

Our car began to move forward again. We had gone only a few yards when Mom said we could get up. Full of excitement, we crawled out from under the blankets and back up and onto the back seat. We were all smiles.

Mom was smiling too.

I can remember looking out the back window of the car and seeing a parking lot full of cars that were full of families—moms and dads with their youngsters in the back, smiling and laughing and eating popcorn.

I was pulled out of my happy thoughts by the sound of Mom asking me to hand her the big sack with the food. I did as I was told only to have her open the bag and find the sandwiches smashed.

For a moment, I thought Mom would lose it as usual, but she surprised me by remaining calm. With a funny look on her face, she inspected the bag and its contents and quickly seemed to realize that the smashed sandwiches were her fault—she had been the one who told us to get down on the floor, forgetting that the sack was already there.

"They'll still eat," she said.

And she was right.

We ate the sandwiches, drank the pop, and had a rare night at the movies that I still remember with fondness. I can't recall what movie was showing on the big screen, but as it began, I do remember seeing Mom scoot closer to the stranger as he slipped his arm around her. From the back seat, I couldn't see her face but I knew without question that she was smiling, and I would give anything to have the memory of her face in that moment. I like to believe that for once, my mother felt safe, content, and worthy of love.

That night was one of those times when life was as it should be.

We were happy together.

Happy
I'm sorry I'm a burden
It was wrong for me to do
I thought you had the answer
I hoped you'd fix me too
What was dark is now in light
The peace I was looking for
I've had from the beginning
I need it more and more
I've often overlooked it
I've had it from the start
The happiness that I longed for
was hidden in my heart
I need no one to be happy
Happiness comes from me
If I choose to be happy,
then happy I will be

Chapter 14

Dyslexia

My struggles with reading date back to my childhood. I spent most of my time in school doing everything I could to avoid it. This had little to do with reading per se and more to do with my troubles when it came to reading.

The first couple of years in school, I loved sitting in a circle listening to my teacher read to me and my classmates. And I don't recall having any trouble reading short individual words on note cards then, either.

But by the time I entered second grade, it was clear to me and everyone else that I had significant difficulties with reading. In the early 1970s, it was common for the teacher to ask the class to follow along in their own books while students took turns reading the story aloud. The first time my teacher did this, I can still recall how my heart began to race.

I did my best to follow along, placing my finger under each word, sliding it from left to right as my classmates took turns reading from the book. But by the time it was my turn, I was kneeling in my seat and doing my best not to run from the classroom.

This became routine.

I was almost always able to read and pronounce the first few words correctly, but after that—no matter how hard I tried, I could not make sense of what I was seeing on the page. I would make a mistake. And then another.

With each mistake, I became more frustrated, which only made reading more difficult.

At some point, my efforts to sound out a simple word would trigger laughter. The teacher always told the students to stop, but by then, the damage had been done.

By the middle of second grade, I not only hated reading, but I also thought I might be stupid. I vowed that my classmates would never laugh at me again, and from that day forward, I refused to read aloud in class. If a teacher tried to force me, I would misbehave until I was banished from the classroom. That might sound extreme to some people, but I suspect only to those who have never faced public ridicule.

By the time I was in third grade, the cake was cooked. I had decided that I was stupid, and I thought there was no hope for me because almost every subject by then, except maybe art, required reading proficiency.

No wonder I hated school.

My teachers' solution was to tell me to practice at home, but there was no adult at home willing to help me with my homework much less my reading. I don't recall any relative ever reading to me either but then maybe they couldn't read themselves. I can't say for sure.

My teachers did try. I was placed in a special reading class, a class that, I'm sad to say, did not help. Every technique offered proved unsuccessful, and so as I grew, my reading skills lagged further and further behind those of my classmates.

My inability to read like everyone else took its toll on me. I would spend the next eight years and two attempts at college convinced that I was too stupid to read well, and assuming I would never be any better at it.

It wasn't until I enrolled at Oklahoma State University in Stillwater, Oklahoma—my third attempt at college—that someone had me tested, and I learned I was dyslexic.

This diagnosis, which is believed to affect as many as 43.5 million Americans, left me overwhelmed with mixed emotions. I didn't know what to think. On one hand, I was happy to know that dyslexia was the cause of my reading issues. On the other hand, I worried that being labeled *dyslexic* would just give people another reason to make fun of me. After all, it is still considered a disability, and people can be cruel.

After my diagnosis, university officials told me I could have help on tests if I wanted; in some cases, I could have people read the test to me. As much as I wanted to use those services, I was too embarrassed to do so. I know that sounds silly now. There is no shame in having a learning condition—any more than there is shame in having a medical condition such as cancer or a broken leg.

But instead, armed with the knowledge that there was a reason reading was difficult for me and I *could* learn, I pushed through college. I often had to read articles, journals, and assignments more than once to absorb the information. When it came to taking quizzes and exams, I was always the last one to complete the test.

But I finished college.

The boy who had always done poorly in school became a young man who averaged almost a 3.5 GPA and made the Dean's List at one of the state's major universities! I went on to pass the tests to become a police officer, and now I'm an author. Who says miracles don't happen?

As I reflect on those horrible early years of school, I only wish someone could have helped me understand what was wrong with me. My teachers did their best—today they would likely have me tested. But back then, all they could do was try to develop my reading skills, and little did they know that only made things worse.

I didn't know how to describe to them what I saw when I looked at the ever-changing letters and words on the page. I never told them the letter "p" might look like a "d" or sometimes a "b." Or that words with repeating letters were especially difficult to read. I see Halloween as *Hallowoeen* and Mississippi as *Missippissi*. When I come across such words, I get completely confused and have to go back and read the whole sentence again—sometimes more than once.

Dyslexia causes me to struggle when typing too. I might type "is" as "si," "but" as "btu," and "are" as "aer." Spell-check will underline what I've typed, but when I look at the words, they look fine to me. I have an extreme-ly difficult time proofreading anything I have written.

Sometimes my dyslexia causes me to leave out words in a sentence, and I don't notice their absence because my brain automatically puts the words in so that what I read looks exactly like what I thought I wrote. I might type: "Today I took my kids the park." Although the word "to" is obviously missing to most people, I see it as if the word "to" is there—my brain places it in its proper place, so when I read back over what I've typed, I have no idea that the sentence is missing a word and is incorrect.

I have learned to compensate for this.

I have learned to slow down and go back over my work, but I also have learned to let others read what I write or type—I now appreciate a good proofreader!

And, yes, being dyslexic remains frustrating, if only because I know that it will never go away. However, I take great joy knowing that I am not dumb. What I would give to go back in time and have one of my teach-ers say to me, "Alton, your inability to read like the other students is because you are dyslexic. You are not dumb! Your brain just scrambles words and letters, and we can help with that!"

The good news: Reading therapy is now available for kids with dyslexia.

Sometimes I Lose Myself
Sometimes I lose myself
Trying to just fit in
When I find a clique

I lose myself again
It's hard to be myself
Trying to be a friend
Authentic is difficult
But easy to pretend
I want to be myself
That's who I should be
Sometimes I lose myself
Trying to just be me

Chapter 15

He Missed Out

I had just finished telling three hundred elementary school students about some of what I had faced during my childhood.

Now it was time for their questions.

As students raised their hands to be called on, the principal handed one after the other the microphone and asked them to stand so everyone could hear their questions. After answering a few dozen questions, I saw a boy take the mic only to have him ask what I now know most people want to ask me: "Where is your father?"

It's funny. Everyone asks me this—old people, young people, rich people, poor people, foster kids, kids with big wonderful dads and families. Children in particular seem desperate to know. Still, I can see in their faces that most of them fear my answer.

On this particular day, I explained to the students that I did not know where my father was because my father had left my mother before I was born.

"I not only do not know my father," I said, "but his name is not even on my birth certificate."

Truth be told, I don't even know the man's name.

As I said, I have been asked and have answered this same question many times over the years, but for some reason, on this day, my voice cracked during my response. I did my best to hold my emotions in, but I knew my words sounded heavy with regret and sadness.

As I finished my reply, the hand of a little blond third-grader in the back of the auditorium popped up. The principal spotted him and headed his way with the microphone, but before the principal could reach him, the boy scooted out of his seat and made the long walk to the front of the auditorium where I stood.

When the boy reached me, he looked me in the eyes and held a hand up for the mic.

I handed it over.

He then reached up and placed his free hand on my shoulder.

My heart began to race. I saw several ways this could go horribly wrong. My biggest fear: The little boy would open up and share a tragic personal story of how he was being abused by his foster family or had been neglected by his dad only to be laughed at by his classmates—or worse yet, teased or rejected by them later after I left.

I held my breath and told myself that if he started to say something he might regret later, I would grab the mic and do what I had to do to clean up whatever response his words generated from the student body.

As those thoughts swirled in my head, the little boy took a deep breath and with great confidence said, "I know you never got a chance to meet your dad, but I want to tell you that I think he missed out."

The little boy then handed me the microphone and made his way back to his seat.

The auditorium fell silent. I stood before them trying to find the courage to respond to this unexpected declaration and the strength to hold back tears.

I looked to the back of the room where the little boy now sat. "Thank you," I said, "I needed to hear that."

Sensing that my talk was over, the principal thanked the students for being a great audience and released them to return to class. I packed up my stuff and fled to my car as fast as I could.

Once safely in my car, I cried tears of joy, tears of truth—because the little boy was right, my dad had missed out.

My dad robbed himself of the joy of standing next to me and saying, "That's my son." But he also stole from me the right to say, "That's my dad."

Open the Door
If it's too good to be true
It's a mirage
Stay on course
Resist self-sabotage

Run from negative thoughts
Keep them out of your head
Don't settle for lies
Think positive instead

When traveling to Peace
You will pass by Shame
It knows you well
And calls you by name

Farther down the road
Is the neighborhood of Hate
You will be tempted
Don't open the gate

And over the hill
You'll think you are clear
The fork in the road
Is Doubt and Fear

Now cut your own road
It's hard at the start
It will take all you have
And require all your heart

The journey's not over
It's only begun
The city of Peace
Has room for just one

THE BOY WHO SURVIVED

You'll pass by Guilt
Who's standing with Pride
They're out in the open
There's nowhere to hide

You can't go around
It's something you must do
To reach your destination
You have to go through

You're sure to get tired
When the pain sets in
Rest on faith not fear
For you will need it to win

Don't look back
Ignorance is bliss
Keep telling yourself
I got this

When that journey is over
There's sure to be more
When opportunity knocks
Open the door

Chapter 16

Discovering Christmas

During the early years of my life, I am certain I did not know what Christmas was, and I for sure did not understand the true meaning of Christmas.

What I had heard about was Santa Claus and how he came down people's chimneys on Christmas Eve and left presents under the tree while everyone was sleeping. The only problem with this scenario was that in all my life, Santa had never once come to our house.

Of course, we didn't have a chimney or a Christmas tree, for that matter. And from what I understood, Santa had a naughty-or-nice list he checked, and he gave gifts only to little boys and girls who were good, for goodness' sake. The Carter children were anything but good, so none of us were all that surprised when Santa Claus failed to ever make an appearance at our house.

In my early childhood, the closest experience to Christmas joy I had ever seen happened the first of every month when Mom's welfare check and food stamps arrived in the mail.

For me, Santa did not travel through the night sky in a red sleigh pulled by reindeer. He drove a white box-shaped truck with the words *U.S. Postal Service* on the side. My Santa did not wear red pants and a fur-trimmed robe. He sported a blue shirt and slacks with a navy stripe running down the sides.

With the arrival of a new month, my siblings and I turned into sentries. As soon as we saw the mail truck enter our neighborhood or apartment complex, one of us would wake Mom and tell her the mailman was here. Mom would then pick one of us to retrieve the mail—the unspoken hope being that her check and food stamps would soon be in the mailbox.

I always felt special when Mom picked me to go get the mail on those days, and I think my siblings did too.

What I also remember is how we all feared the days when the postman did not deliver. Mom's irritability would grow and sometimes turn into anger. I realize now she was like a desperate bird with hungry babies in the nest, mouths agape, squawking for food. Getting that check guaranteed that we would eat again—at least for the next week or so. Its arrival also triggered the next phase of our monthly ritual: acquiring transportation.

Given that we had no car and public transportation was basically nonexistent in our town, Mom would first have to find somebody with a car to take her to cash her government check. Then, she would often need to find someone else to take her to the grocery store so she could purchase food with the food stamps—and if they couldn't stick around, she might have to find someone else to bring her back home. If no one was available to take Mom, we did it as a family: We walked.

Being poor is hard work.

Ours was not the lovely holiday shopping experience one associates with Christmas—or any day of the year for that matter. Mom did not like taking us with her to the grocery store; we always asked for things and often acted out to boot. Going alone, however, was not an option for her. She needed help carrying the bags of groceries home.

My favorite part of the monthly ritual was putting up the groceries. I loved unpacking the cans and boxes from the brown paper sacks, handing them to Mom to put away, and watching the empty cabinets and refrigerator fill back up. After we were done, Mom would usually retreat to her bedroom, but I often went back to the kitchen so I could open the cabinets one by one and look at all the food on the nicely filled shelves.

Mom always seemed to be her happiest at the beginning of the month, but as the days passed and the food dwindled, so did her patience and mood.

At various times throughout the year, however, Good Samaritans from school or church would occasionally bring that special-first-of-the-month joy to the house in the form of brown paper sacks filled with groceries—quieting our hunger pains and lifting Mom's blues, if only for a day or two.

Unfortunately, I don't think the message Mom took away from such visits is what the Good Samaritans had in mind. One evening about eight o'clock while my siblings and I were playing in our living room, there was a knock at the front door. I heard Mom wonder aloud who could possibly be coming around this late, cycling through all the most likely candidates.

Finally, she got up to see who it was.

I will never forget looking past Mom that night and seeing one of my teachers holding two brown paper sacks. Mom and my teacher exchanged a few words, and then Mom stepped aside, and in came my teacher and three other women, also holding grocery sacks. I watched my mom's face tighten with what even I recognized as embarrassment. I know now that came from not only the condition of our home but also the reason for our unexpected guests' visit.

As for our guests, they couldn't hide their shock as they entered and took in the state of the living room on their way to the kitchen.

"Hello, Alton," my teacher said with a small smile. "How are you doing?"

"I'm fine," I said, knowing that any minute a roach or empty refrigerator could make a liar out of me.

The women deposited the sacks on the dirty counter in the kitchen and then moved to leave, once again seeming to take in the condition of our house as if they couldn't believe what their eyes were seeing.

On the front porch, they paused to say goodbye. Mom stood in the doorway. "Thank you for the food," she said.

Behind her, I whispered to my brother, "I knew it! They brought us food!"

"How do you know it's food in the sacks?" he whispered back.

"I saw a loaf of bread sticking out of one of the bags," I said as I heard Mom thank the women a second time. Then she closed the door and looked right at me: "The only reason your teacher brought us food is because she and those other women feel sorry for us."

I can still recall how her pain and shame washed over me that night as she brushed by me on her way to the kitchen. She put up the groceries and then came and found me again. "How did they know we didn't have any food, Alton?" she asked.

"I didn't say a word!" I said.

The look on her face said she did not believe me.

"Alton, did you tell your teachers we didn't have any food?" she asked again. "Because you should know that DHS is now going to come take all of you away."

And then Mom repeated the phrase I had already heard a thousand times before in my young life. "White people, teachers, and police officers cannot be trusted," she said. "All they want to do is take all of you away from me."

This was something our mom told us on a regular basis, although I never did understand why. For one, what she said did not make sense to me.

The very people whom my mom seemed to despise or didn't trust were the only people who had ever seemed to care about me or be concerned about whether I was fed or safe or getting enough sleep. But my mother seemed convinced that such people brought us food only so they could spy on us—and then report back to the Department of Human Services or the school. Maybe she was right but I didn't think so. I thought they were just trying to do what they could to help.

And as for Mom telling me that my teachers brought us food only because they felt sorry for us, well, my stomach didn't know the difference.

Ghetto Claus

Twas the day before Xmas and all through the FLC*
not a member was stirring as far as we could see
The chairs were stacked in the closet with care
in hopes that Mr. Claus would soon be there

The youth were all home asleep in their beds
while visions of chocolate danced in their heads
When out of nowhere there came such a clatter
I sprang from my office to see what was the matter

I ran to the window cause I thought I'd heard shooting
But I had just fallen asleep and only was tooting
I looked to the ghetto and what did appear
a tricked-out sleigh and eight rapping reindeer

With a crazy old driver so laid back with pause
I could tell by his music it must be Ghetto Claus
More rapid than text messaging his eight reindeer came
and he beatboxed a rap and called them by name

THE BOY WHO SURVIVED

Now T-bone, now Lavaun, now Leshea and Tyrone
on Jermaine, on Shanell, on Quita and Dramone
They crashed into the porch and hit the wall hard
dash away homies the police they'll call

Up to the housetop the reindeer they flew
with a sleigh full of toys and Ghetto Claus too
And just like that I heard on the roof
the reindeer were dancing with spinners on each hoof

I couldn't believe it when I turned around
in the front door Claus himself came with a bound
Dressed in fur except for one thing
around his neck gold-plated bling

And that's when I saw it was not the toys on his back
I knew it! I knew it! Ghetto Claus is black!
A twinkle from his grill and a twist of his head
soon let me know I had nothing to dread.

He said *waz up* and went straight to work
filled each stocking and then turned with a jerk
He sprang to his sleigh without wasting any time
and away they flew as they turned on a dime

I heard his bass as he flew out of sight
Merry Christmas to all and to all a good night!

*Family Lice Center

Chapter 17

Positive Tomorrows

A few years ago, after my first book, *The Boy Who Carried Bricks*, came out, I received an invitation to visit the students of Positive Tomorrows in Oklahoma City, Oklahoma. The invitation came from a third-grade teacher who had read my book and believed my story might resonate with her students.

I knew I had to go.

Positive Tomorrows is the only elementary school in Oklahoma created to serve homeless children.

Founded in 1990 with support from the Mayor's Task Force on Homelessness, Oklahoma City Public Schools, Junior League of Oklahoma City, YWCA Oklahoma City, Neighborhood Services Organization, Campfire, and United Way of Central Oklahoma, the school started as a satellite of OKCPS, with more than half of its funding coming from the Oklahoma Department of Education. In 2006, when that funding was lost in the aftermath of the passage of No Child Left Behind, the local community rallied behind the school and its students. Positive Tomorrows reopened the following year as a private, tuition-free elementary school.

It has remained open ever since.

By the time of my visit to Positive Tomorrows, I had spoken at schools both big and small across Oklahoma and the nation, but never at a school in which every single student was homeless.

I was ever so curious as to why I was there.

The teacher who had invited me to the school met me out front. She thanked me for making the trip and agreeing to speak to her students. "You have lots in common with my students," she said over and over again. "I hope meeting you will inspire them not to give up."

After giving me a quick tour of the small school and introducing me to several of her fellow teachers, she showed me to her classroom. We found the students sitting on the floor in a circle waiting for us.

"Students, this is my friend Alton Carter. He's an author. He came by to say hi—so if all of you would remain seated, he is going to join us and share a little bit of his story," the teacher said.

She grabbed a chair, placed it in front of the students, and told me I could begin.

I took it slow. I showed them my book. I shared a few stories from my childhood. And then I mentioned that I did not know who my father was—not even his name.

A hush fell over the room.

Several of the children spoke up at that point. They told me that they had never met their dads either. In that exchange, a connection was forged. I finished sharing my story and joined the children on the floor.

It was now the teacher's turn to talk. She told the children that she had asked me to come visit their school because she wanted them to all see that they could be like me and become whatever they wanted to be—no matter what they had been through.

"Do you have any questions for Mr. Carter?"

Without a word, one of the boys stood, walked around the outside of the circle, and stopped beside me. I was still sitting with his classmates on the floor. He bent down as if to whisper in my ear only to say in a low voice that only I could hear, "I wish you were my dad."

He stood right back up and stared at me as if waiting for a response. Caught off guard and unsure of what to say in the moment, I followed my instincts—I put my arm around his shoulders and pulled him in for a hug as I looked at the teacher in amazement.

"What did he say?" she asked.

I told her that he wished I was his dad.

The boy started to walk away, and I pulled him back, looked him in the eye, and said, "I wish I was your dad because you are a great kid."

After hearing my response, the student walked back around the circle and sat back down in his original spot. As soon as he was seated another student, a little girl, said, "I wish you were my dad too."

The teacher quickly jumped in and told the students it was time to return to their desks and get out their science projects. Over the next hour, I went around and spent one-on-one time with every student in the class until the teacher said it was time for recess. She invited me to join them, and I accepted, following the class outside. The playground wasn't very big but had everything kids need to burn off energy.

What I did find unusual was the tall privacy fence that ringed the playground. Puzzled, I asked the teacher about it. She told me it was for the children's protection. On the front of the school, a small sign identifies it as Positive Tomorrows, and because so many people know the school is for homeless children the school administrators wanted to make sure the students' privacy was protected. Hence, the fence.

As the teacher finished, the principal appeared and asked if she could give me a tour of the school. I followed her into the building where we peeked our heads into each classroom to say hello. After that, she showed me the school pantry full of toiletries, clothes, and hair products for the students.

We then made our way into the small counselor's office where I noticed several cots placed around the room. I knew they were for sleeping but couldn't help asking why the cots were there. Were they for when children got sick? The principal said yes and no. She then explained that many of their students came to school having been up all night. Her words reminded me all too well of how Uncle Stevie used to keep my cousins and me up late on school nights and how the next day at school, I would have to fight to keep my eyes open.

I remembered getting in trouble for that.

Suddenly, the cots took on a whole different meaning for me. You see at Positive Tomorrows instead of punishing children who fall asleep in class or sending them to the office, students are sent to the counselor's office where they can sleep as long as they need.

Hearing the principal say that made me realize that my teachers never asked me why I was tired or sleepy. Not once as far as I can recall. Instead, they usually got upset with me and sent me to the office. But I am also pretty sure if they had asked, I would not have told them that I hadn't slept because there had been an all-night party at my house or I was afraid to fall asleep because of all the roaches. Still, it sure would have been nice if one of them had asked me *why* I was falling asleep, just once.

We finished the tour, and I thanked her again for the privilege of visiting their school.

I drove the little over an hour back to Stillwater and arrived to find an email from the third-grade teacher who had invited me to Positive Tomorrows:

> After you left our class, I asked one of my students if he was going to be like Alton and be the first person in his family to graduate from high school and he replied, *If I live long enough.*

Then she wrote:

117

ALTON CARTER

This is why it is so important that people like you share your journey to success with students like mine, so they can have hope.

Sadly, this would not be the last time I heard this from a teacher . . . or a child.

I Am Alton Carter
I was constantly walking on eggshells
There was no one I could tell.

No one cared, so I didn't try
Not disobedience just a hopeless cry.

Always hungry, always cold
It will always be this way is what I was told.

I won't be like my family; it's not right
No abuse, cursing, or starting fights.

My situation's not a setback; it'll only push me harder
I am Alton Carter.

—written by Braily Perchiful
Mrs. Eden's class, Bristow Middle School
Bristow, Oklahoma

Chapter 18

Why He Stayed

This is a question I have pondered for more than forty years: Why did Grandpa stay?

As a little boy, I often got up when my grandfather did and watched him get ready for another day of toil before the sun had lit up the neighborhood. From the living-room window, I watched him back his truck out of the driveway and disappear over the hill to work.

When I could no longer see the taillights of his truck, I would return to my sleeping spot on the floor, all the while trying to figure out why he would ever come back.

I was certain Grandpa went to work to escape the chaos that consumed his house. And many a night, he did not return from work until long after dark.

But he always came back.

Why?

I could think of a hundred good reasons why he should have left never to return. His family brought him far more pain than peace, as far as I could see. My uncles were nothing more than squatters who lived rent free while filling their stomachs with food they never lifted a finger to buy. I never saw my uncles physically harm Grandpa, but they did not mince words when they had something horrible to say to their father.

My mom had a toxic relationship with both of my grandparents. Yet somehow always found a way to smooth things over with them long enough to drop us off at their house on the weekend. Mom and Grandma always fought after her return, usually because my mother was often hours or even days late coming back to get us.

As for Grandma, well, my grandparents had times when they looked as if they enjoyed each other's company but too often they slung hateful words and accusations at each other. They mostly fought about my uncles. Grandma blindly loved her sons and went to great lengths to defend and protect them from any criticism— even constructive criticism, even fair concerns my grandfather had about the way his sons were living their lives.

And then there were their seven grandchildren. Grandchildren are supposed to be a blessing, but we were dropped off at my grandparent's house like dirty laundry. And that is how we felt—like an unwanted basket of filthy clothes. We only added to the burden Grandpa already carried. Except for my grandparents, everyone living in their house not only consumed all available resources but were also constantly in some sort of trouble.

Their sons and daughters were in trouble with the police or on drugs. Their grandchildren were in trouble at school or in the neighborhood, and that included me.

We had little respect for authority.

My siblings and I moving into my grandparents' house only added another act to what was already a three-ring circus. With the living room as the center ring, we saw violence, alcohol, drugs, and stolen property bring local law enforcement to see the show too often. Adults think children are oblivious to what is going on, and it is true that *normal* is often defined by what you know, but I can also tell you that children *know* when their house has become a place of fear and derision in the neighborhood.

There is no way our family could have survived without my grandpa, and we all knew it. Grandpa worked three jobs to pay the bills, and he was handy enough to fix almost anything that needed to be repaired around the house. He usually had three grown sons living under his roof, but not a one lifted a hand to help—not by getting a job but also not by helping with chores or repairs. There are many ways to contribute to a family's well-being, but I don't recall my uncles ever offering to pitch in. So Grandpa worked at home and then went to work and then returned to more work. He must have been so weary.

Why did Grandpa return to the three-ring circus every evening?

Why did he stay?

Four decades passed before I got my answer. And when that answer came, it was from a fourth-grader in

Edmond, Oklahoma. I had just shared my story in an all-school assembly, and the principal had made arrangements for me to stop by several classrooms so I could take questions from the students. My first stop was a large room where two fourth-grade classes had gathered. I took a seat in a small plastic chair and quickly recapped some of the low points of my childhood.

As soon as I finished sharing, a student who had positioned himself in the middle of the room raised his hand.

I asked, "Do you have a question?"

He replied, "I do have a question."

I gave him a nod to go ahead.

"Mr. Carter, you told us that your dad did not stick around to take care of you, but can you tell us why your grandpa stayed?"

For a minute, his words left me speechless. He'd asked the million-dollar question. I finally replied, "I have thought about that question for years, and honestly I don't know why my grandpa stayed."

The room went silent.

In that silence, many reasons why my grandfather should have left came to mind—but not a single answer as to why he returned to the little house in Stillwater every night. My thoughts were interrupted by an under-sized African-American boy who was sitting at the back of the room.

"I know why he stayed," the little boy said.

Filled with curiosity and a little bit of fear, I asked him why he thought my grandpa stayed all those years. I was certain he didn't have a clue and that his answer would leave the rest of the kids and possibly me only more confused. But to my surprise, he delivered an explanation that was more than plausible.

"I think your grandpa stayed to take care of the kids."

"Excuse me?" I said.

The little boy repeated his theory: "Your grandpa stayed to take care of you, your brothers and sisters, and your cousins." And then the little boy said, "I think he stayed because he wanted to make sure you had a place to stay and food to eat."

After years of wondering why, I finally had an answer to one of the biggest mysteries in my life. I could not see my face when the answer was revealed to me, but I am sure it lit up like a light bulb. My grandpa had passed on many years ago, so I couldn't ask him if what the little boy that day said was true, but his was the first reason that had ever made sense to me: Grandpa stayed because he cared.

I finished the question-and-answer session, and as the students filed out of the room, I approached the little boy who had so matter-of-factly solved one of the great mysteries of my life. I thanked him for what he had said and shook his hand. As he disappeared down the hall with his class, he left me with a renewed sense of peace.

I can now tell people my grandpa stayed for me.

Thomas L. Carter
I've had this question for years
You've always been strong
I never saw your tears

You deserved better
So why did you stay
You always came back
When most ran away

You came home each night
You always paid the bills
You made an honest living
When others sold pills

We all mistreated you
Didn't realize what we had
All of us were selfish
Couldn't tell that you were sad

So all these years
And through all the drama
Why did you stay
In a house full of trauma

You should have left
Without a goodbye
We thought you would leave
Without a goodbye

Instead you stayed
You stayed till the end
And I never asked why
Why did you stay

Please tell me why
I have my suspicions
And maybe I'm wrong
I had every chance to ask
But waited too long

So thank you for building
The roof over my head
Thank you for staying
To make sure we were fed

I'm glad that you stayed
You were the knot in my rope
You were all that I had
My hero, my hope

Chapter 19

Things I Didn't Know

What we know about life is rooted in what we see in our own life and home. And what we consider normal tends to be defined by what we know or have experienced ourselves.

We might catch a glimpse of how other people live at school or church or on TV or in the movies, but for most people, what comprises a *normal family* or *normal childhood* is their family or their childhood.

We don't even know what we don't know.

I know I didn't.

And almost every single day, I run into someone who finds it difficult to grasp all the things I just didn't know . . . as a child, as a teen, as a young man, and even as a husband and certainly as a father. My list is pretty darn long but nowhere near complete.

ALTON CARTER

What I Didn't Know
I didn't know kids could have their own bed.
Didn't know people had pantries stocked with food.
Didn't know people had checking accounts.
Didn't know people had driver's licenses.
Didn't know you were supposed to have car insurance.
Didn't know people lived places for more than six months
at a time.

I thought everybody had roaches in their house.
Thought everybody lied.
Thought everybody stole things.
Thought everybody drank alcohol.
Thought everybody did drugs.
Thought all men beat women.

I didn't know people had washing machines.
Didn't know you could trust police.
Didn't know you could trust teachers.
Didn't know you could trust social workers.
Didn't know parents read to their kids.
Didn't know you could have more than one item for a meal.
Didn't know people had matching plates and cups.
Didn't know people sat down to eat meals at a table.

I thought everybody went to the emergency room instead
of the doctor when ill or hurt.
Thought everybody abused their children.
Thought everybody put alcohol in their baby's bottles.

Thought everybody cussed.
Thought social workers came to everybody's house.
Thought everybody had been to jail.
Thought only blacks were on welfare.
Thought everybody went to church only on Easter.
Thought everybody had an outie belly button.
Thought everybody got their utilities cut off.

I didn't know people ate three meals a day.
Didn't know bath water should be nice and warm.
Didn't know children took their dad's last name.
Didn't know people went on vacation.
Didn't know parents should protect their children.
Didn't know smoking and drinking were unhealthy.

I didn't know it was normal for babies to cry.
Didn't know why mom settled for abusive men.
Didn't know kids had birthday parties.
Didn't know how to argue without getting physical.
Didn't know who my dad was.
Didn't know my home life wasn't normal.
Didn't know I would need counseling.
Didn't know how strong I was.
Didn't know what trust was.
Didn't know one day I would find love.
Didn't know I would—or could—build my own family.

Chapter 20

My Wife

In 1978, I stood in a courtroom and heard a judge tell my mother she was unfit to raise her five children. In that moment, I made a promise to myself that a judge would never tell me I was unfit to be a father.

I had no idea how or when I would get my chance to prove I could be a good father to the world, but that day in court made me determined to do what had eluded almost everyone in my family.

I took what guidance I could from their example, mostly from Grandpa's. And I looked elsewhere.

In the years I was shuffled from foster home to foster home, I had a chance to see how couples celebrated good times and survived bad times. I saw how they fought, solved problems, and dealt with tragedy, both big and small.

Every couple I lived with had their own way of dealing with the highs and lows of life, but I came to realize
that in the end—no matter how they got there and even
if they had had to argue the whole way—they ultimately
ended up on the same page. More important, they did so
without abusing each other physically or verbally.

That gave me hope.

As long as I could remember, I had dreamed of the
day when I would come home after a long hard day's
work and be greeted with hugs by my wife and kids. I
imagined us taking turns talking about our day and then
washing up for a family meal. When dinner was over, I
saw us spending a few hours together in the living room
before baths and bedtime.

That was my dream.

Truth be told, I couldn't wait to prove my worth to
the amazing woman who would give me the chance to be
a husband and father . . . who would help me make the
family that I had always wanted.

And I finally found that amazing woman.

Her name is Kristin.

As for marriage and family, well, that reality proved
to be a little more challenging than I had expected. No
matter how hard I tried, being married was not that simple, and parenting was far more complicated than I could
ever have imagined.

As for my relationship with Kristin, we had our struggles. My wife comes from a small town, and she grew up
with her siblings and both parents all under the same
roof. Kristin's parents also protected her, supported her,

and did whatever they could to show their love for her—they were great parents, and they raised a woman with one of the most generous hearts I've ever known.

My upbringing, on the other hand, could not have been more different than my wife's. And for a very long time, I tried to hide the truth about my childhood from Kristin—not because I wanted to deceive her but because I was afraid she could never love me for who I was and where I came from if she knew.

To make matters worse, it did not take long for my biological family to insert themselves into our relationship. They were soon calling Kristin and asking for money, food, clothes, and rides to various places. Kristin never seemed to mind, but her efforts to help my family made me resent them more than I already did.

After dating for years, we decided that we wanted to get married. I never gave her the fairy-tale proposal she deserved and gave her the only ring I could afford. And when the topic of my asking her father for her hand in marriage came up, I refused for three reasons.

1. I was afraid to ask him.

2. I was convinced that he would say no and tell her that I wasn't good enough for her.

And 3. I didn't want him to ask me questions for which I didn't have the answers, questions like *What are you going to do to support your family?*

Despite this, we eventually did marry. Her parents did their part with the wedding while I struggled to accept their role as my in-laws. I also remained uncomfortable in my new role as a husband.

We got off to a bad start, and things quickly became complicated. I was not prepared to be married. I made so many horrible decisions. I quit jobs on a whim, left the house in the middle of arguments, and too often acted or responded out of fear. My insecurities also caused me to continue to resent the close relationship she had with her parents. But Kristin stuck with me through it all.

And slowly but surely, we figured out marriage.

My Wife
I'm happy when you're happy
I'm sad when you are sad
I laugh when you laugh
Wait. I'm always mad

You are quirky and stubborn
And you are not the talker
You fall asleep on a dime
You are a Facebook stalker

You love reading at night
And the Lifetime network
You're stuck with a mess
It should be a perk

You love sleeping in
You love family trips
You love Italian food
You love salty chips

You love hot tamales
You love Diet Coke
You love movie popcorn
You can't tell a joke

You love your children
You love back rubs
You don't like Sam's
You like BDubs

You love Chex Mix
You love your spouse
You love alone time
You'd like a clean house

You love being home
You love ice tea
You really love chocolate
Thanks for loving me

Chapter 21

My Family

When my children were born, I was filled with equal amounts of joy and doubt. I wanted more than anything to be the world's greatest dad, the father I never had.

I wanted my children to be proud of me.

I wanted their love.

And their respect.

But I had no idea how to go about being a good father. I was completely inconsistent when it came to discipline. And too often, I tried to win their love with gifts. It took a while for me to learn that kids don't need *things* to be happy—they need *you.*

They need *time with you.*

I had always dreamed of living in a home where the people love and respect each other. This was my chance.

And I refused to blow it.

Looking back, I realize now that because I wanted a loving, supportive family so much, I thought it would be easy to do. With the passage of time, however, I came to realize that creating a family is easy; living together as a family is hard.

Much of what I eventually learned about being a father and my role in the family came from Kristin and my two boys—and the example Kristin's parents set, especially her father. I had never seen a good father being a father up close, watching Kristin and her dad interact was a good place to start.

Over the years, I learned how important it is to be honest with those I love while also being honest with myself. I also learned that running away when Kristin and I disagree might keep us from screaming at each other, but it only kicks the can of communication—and whatever the problem is—down the road.

As for my fears about being a father, they slowly faded away once I realized that my children would love me regardless of my past or which family tree I had fallen from. As for my dreams of being the perfect father, they faded away too when I learned that my children didn't want me to be perfect.

They just need me to be present.

To this very day, my relationship with Kristin is far from perfect—and she'd be the first to admit that, but what matters is that we are still together.

What keeps us together is our love for each other. Love helps us survive the bad times, and love allows us to cherish the good times.

I stay.

She stays.

It is as simple as that. And unlike with my grandpa and grandma, I don't think our children will ever have reason to ask *why* we stayed. And I take comfort in that.

By 2017, our two sons, Kelton and Colin, were fast becoming young men. Time goes so fast. The Carter nest would soon be empty.

We decided to fill it. We had love to spare.

Over the course of a year or so, we met and adopted three siblings from a home for abused children based in Arkansas. In the end, the love and joy that Kelton and Colin had given us as parents gave Kristin and me the strength and courage to welcome Alliyah, Angilina, and Curtis into our family.

They had been in the foster system for several years by the time we met them. I'm sure during that time they had dreamed, as so many foster kids do, about having a home again, but that didn't mean the transition from foster care to our home was an easy one. It wasn't. There were many long days and traumatic nights after the three of them moved in. Love alone cannot heal everything that a child who has been abused comes with, but it sure is a good place to start.

The three of them have been more than a blessing—for us, and also for our friends. Thanks to people such as Janelda and David Lane, our children have a support system that won't waver in the strongest of winds, a village of folks who have their best interests at heart. People who want to help them heal so that one day when they are grown and ready, Alliyah, Angilina, and Curtis can make our Carter family even larger, with loving families of their own.

There's no one-size-fits-all recipe for creating a happy family. It is rarely easy, and even on the best of days, it takes hard work and patience. As with a good marriage, a family requires compromise and people who love each other more than themselves. But thanks to my wife and children, I have become the father I never had. And I am married to a woman who devotes all her energy to her family. And yes, there are times when we don't get along, but there are also times when we can't wait to see each other. There are times when our children drive us nuts and times when they make us feel like superheroes.

Marriage and parenting can be like juggling plates while riding a unicycle blindfolded. You can hope against hope that you won't make a fool of yourself, but odds are that you're bound to run into or over something and crash, dropping every plate. What makes having a family so great is that when your circus act takes an unexpected turn to disaster, someone is there to pick you up.

That's family.

It's about creating memories that can be remembered and passed down one generation to the next. It's about sharing your life with someone in the hopes of growing old together. Meeting Kristin was a big step toward having the family I always dreamed about, but it wasn't the first step. That came many, many years earlier when as a little boy, I found the courage to walk away from my grandparents' home, away from my given family, believing deep inside that I deserved a family that was about love and not abuse—and determined to do whatever it took to make that a reality.

My hopes of having a happy home with a wife and children of my own came true because I finally chose to believe that even someone like me deserves love.

And if I can make marriage and a family work, so can you. Just remember these five things:

1. There are no perfect people. Making a marriage work requires you to work on yourself *and* your marriage.

2. Learn to forgive and to let things go.

3. Try each day to be a better you.

4. Put your family's needs above your wants.

5. Do the best that you can until you know better. Once you know better, do better.

I Know My Role
Now that I'm better
I finally understand

My role is to love you
the best way I can

I need to be present
without asking why

Be there to listen
give a shoulder on which to cry

I need to remind you
you're beautiful and smart

Show you you're special
and how to follow your heart

To give you your space
and wait by the phone

To text you good morning
when you feel alone

I'm really protective
I'm not sure why

Sometimes I'm nosy
I don't mean to pry

You make me happy
that's always the case

There's no better picture
than when I see your face

Chapter 22

Hold It Together

Most days in the lives of most people are good—or at least uneventful. If something bad should happen, whatever the problem, it is usually a temporary state of affairs. And the light at the end of the proverbial tunnel is almost always within sight . . . for most people.

That was not my experience as a child.

And I know that's not true of so many children living a version of my childhood now.

And although there are many good people—teachers, coaches, police officers, ministers, neighbors, librarians, social workers—who want to help when they find a child or family in such need, most cannot understand how persistent and continual and frightening the needs of a child or family in crisis are. A sack of groceries is always welcome, but that food will feed a family of six for what?

A day? Maybe if stretched, a week? Even the latter leaves 345 days of the year. And fifty-one other weeks.

That is a lifetime to a child.

I believe that's also why children living in such a home are to be admired, not pitied. These children must carry on whether or not a Good Samaritan shows up on any particular day, even on Christmas . . . sometimes they must hold on for hundreds of other days, year after year after year. They must carry on despite situations and conditions that would make a grown man or woman cry for mercy.

They are why I do what I do.

I was reminded of this during one of my school visits. Several students had gathered at the door of their classroom to welcome me, shake my hand, and tell me how excited they were that I was visiting their school.

I thanked them for having me, and then went desk by desk so I could shake the hands of the rest of the class, and that is when I noticed a student at the back of the classroom.

The little redheaded boy was pacing, with his head down. He had an air of sadness about him. I immediately wanted to go talk with him, but I was afraid that if I did, the rest of the class would follow, and the attention might put him under an unwanted spotlight. Instead, I gave my talk, listened to the students share their own stories, and took some questions—all the while keeping an eye on the little boy, who had yet to take a seat.

During the Q&A, a dozen or more of his fellow students had talked openly about the difficult situations they found themselves in at home or in life. One student had been living in a motel with her mother, but she had recently been taken away by DHS and was now in foster care. Another student shared that he had never met his father because his dad was in prison. And yet another student wasn't sure whether to be happy or scared about being recently adopted.

Eventually our time drew to a close. I thanked the students for sharing and for being respectful to each other in the process. The latter, I have found, is key to creating a safe place where people, both young and old, feel they can talk freely.

It was time for me to go.

But before I could leave, the little boy from the back of the class approached me. I bent down so I could look him in the face: "Is there something you'd like to ask me?"

He nodded vigorously. "I have one question."

He looked around to make sure none of his classmates could hear. When he turned back, he asked, "When you were little, how did you hold yourself together?"

I looked him straight in the eye, pointed at him, and said, "The same way you are holding yourself together . . . one day at a time."

He walked back to his desk with a smile on his face.

He had mastered the secret of survival.

He had learned to hold on . . . one day at a time . . . holding on to the belief that one day life would be better.

He is a survivor.

He is my hero.

The Momentum Way
Strive to be the change
Remember you have a voice
Stand for what you believe
You always have a choice

United when you can
Now is never too late
Be the voice of reason
Leave no room for hate

You are stronger than you know
Choose to do what's right
Remember where you came from
Be a beacon of light

Your past doesn't define you
Make the most of every day
Be strong and never quit
Because that's the Momentum Way

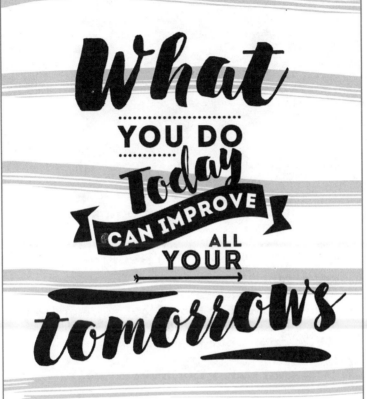

What
YOU DO
Today
CAN IMPROVE
ALL
YOUR
tomorrows

MY JOURNAL

How To Use Your Journal

There is no right or wrong way to use your journal pages.

1. Write down your thoughts — short or long.

2. Write down your poems or songs.

3. Draw your own art or make a list.

4. Answer the questions — or ask your own!

This journal is a place for your dreams and goals and thoughts and musings . . . and each entry will take you closer to who and where you want to be.

—Alton

You have
been given
the heart
of a
champion.

— Alton

Who are you?

We are only
as good as
we make
others feel.

— Alton

What makes you laugh?

What makes you happy?

Things I wish I'd known before today:

You cannot
change the
past no
matter how
many times
you replay it
in your head.

— Alton

Who is your hero? And why?

What makes you, you?

You have to
be clear
about where
you are
to see
where you
are going!

— Alton

sketch spot

What bricks do you carry?

What bricks can you put down?

> Use the bricks you carry to build your foundation for a hopeful future.
>
> — Alton

Who do you need to forgive?

The only
way to heal
a wound
is to make
peace with
the one who
created it.

— Alton

_____

_____

_____

_____

_____

_____

_____

Who do you need to thank?

_____

_____

_____

_____

_____

_____

_____

_____

What is your favorite memory?

Do not let
your pain
from the
past be for
nothing.
Heal — and
use it to
make the
world a
better place.

— Alton

Describe a perfect day.

What is your greatest challenge?

Today I take
back what
was taken
from me
long ago,
and I
determine
how far I
will go.

— Alton

How can you change your life?

How can you change the world?

My journey
to heal is
difficult
and full of
setbacks, but
at the end of
the day, the
difficulties
that come with
healing feel
better than
the pain of
brokenness!

— Alton

What is your biggest dream?

Be the
kid who
dreamed
big.

— Alton

sketch spot

sketch spot

If you were to write a letter, who would it be to . . . and what would you say?

Question: What is the one thing a survivor wants even more than to be loved?

Answer: For the pain to go away!

Losing the pain may
mean having to go
it alone at times
like I did, or sometimes
being alone as I was,
but I promise,
if you work at it every day,
your life will get better.

— Alton

About the Author

Alton Carter is author of the award-winning nonfiction books *The Boy Who Carried Bricks* and *Aging Out* and the picture books *The Boy Who Dreamed Big* and *The Boy Who Went to the Library*. A former foster child and police officer, he is a graduate of Oklahoma State University in Stillwater, Oklahoma, where he makes his home. Leave him a message at www.AltonCarter.net.